SERVANT FIRST

READINGS AND REFLECTIONS ON THE PRACTICE OF SERVANT LEADERSHIP

GRACE PREEDY BARNES

Precedent Press

ISBN: ISBN0-9763088-4-3

Direct correspondence and permission requests to:
    E-mail: orders@precedentpress.org
    Web site: www.precedentpress.org
    Mail: Precedent Press
              9465 Counselors Row, Suite 200
              Indianapolis, Indiana 46240
    Telephone: 317-348-4118

General Editor: Grace Preedy Barnes
Design and layout: Todd Giles of TAGdesign Studios — www.tagdesignstudios.com
Copy Editor: Jack Williams
Education Consultant: Christine Wood
Producer: John Johnson

Cover Image: Scripture verses from chapter 3 of the Gospel of John in various languages.

This reader is dedicated to all to who desire to lead by serving and serve by leading servant leaders at work in the worldwide Kingdom of God.

— *Grace Preedy Barnes*

Table of Contents

Introduction

An Introduction to a Radical Countercultural Style of Leadership

The terms "servant," "servanthood," "service," and "leadership" have been with us for a very long time, especially in Christian environments. Many Christian vocational choices have been made with service as a deep motivation. The Christian is taught at an early age to serve others and that Christ came to serve. To understand the concept of "servant leadership" we must begin by understanding the significance of servanthood and some of the differences between servanthood and service, and servanthood and manipulation. The term "servant leadership" contains paradox and is contradictory in meaning within itself. "Servant" and "leader" are at opposite ends of the hierarchy. Also, "servant" tends to be a soft, more female type of word and "leader" a harder, more male type word. In this combined term the two come together in a holistic form.

The idea of servant is deep in the Judeo-Christian heritage. The Bible lists over 1,300 references to servant, including serve and service. Yet today our societies do not seem to be more caring. There are many great examples that stand out in history, but we live in a day when a leadership that serves seems fuzzier and fuzzier. It may be surprising to many that the term/concept of servant leadership does not come out of religious roots, per se, but a business context. Robert Greenleaf, a Quaker, employed by AT&T for many years, became known there as the resident radical and a general observer of institutions. In the 1950s Greenleaf read a story that profoundly impacted his view of leadership. But this view lay dormant for eleven years until the late 1960s when he felt it could help what he saw was a crisis in leadership. The story that he read was in Hermann Hesse's *Journey to the East*:

> *The term servant leadership contains paradox and is contradictory in meaning within itself.*

"In this story we see a band of men on a mythical journey probably also Hesse's own journey. The central figure of the story is Leo who accompanies the party as the servant who does their menial chores, but who also sustains them with his spirit and his song. He is a person of extraordinary presence. All goes well until Leo disappears. Then the group falls into disarray and the journey is abandoned. They cannot make it without the servant Leo. The narrator, one of the party, after some years of wandering finds Leo and is taken into the Order that had sponsored the journey. There he discovers that Leo, whom he had known first as servant, was in fact the titular head of the Order, its guiding spirit,

a great and noble leader."

Greenleaf gave a number of lectures and wrote essays over the next years that eventually were published in a book called *Servant Leadership* and is now considered the main text on this subject. Several booklets have also been published and the concepts have been applied in many contexts. Greenleaf believes that institutions can serve and be served as well as individuals. He strongly feels that trustees/boards and seminaries have the greatest opportunities to convey vision downward but do not, most of the time, because they are run more like businesses. Trust needs to be established in a body that is separate from management.

> *The idea of servant is deep in Judeo-Christian heritage.*

In a continually changing world, educational, religious, business, and political systems are all in transition. We are told that we are moving into a new era, a great paradigm shift, which is producing unrest, turmoil, and anxiety. The need for strong non-traditional leadership is evident. East is meeting West in our ever-evolving global village, and leadership needs to have a more holistic, group-oriented, cross-cultural vision and worldview.

According to Greenleaf, the servant leader is servant-first and the leadership comes out of the desire to influence. The servant-first and leader-first are two extreme types. The servant-first leader makes sure that other people's highest priority needs are being served. He asks the question:

"Do those served become healthier, wiser, freer, more autonomous, more likely themselves to become servants? And, what is the effect on the least privileged in society; will he benefit or at least, will he not be further deprived?"

In my mind servant leadership is neither prestige ascribed nor prestige achieved, but is rather what someone becomes. This is crucial to grasp because in our task-oriented Western societies we can look at this as something more to work at or achieve. Servant leaders influence by example, by their presence, and persuasion.

I believe that the concepts of servant leadership can be biblical or non-biblical and used by Christians or non-Christians. The non-Christian motivation, I think, still has the organization's success in mind, so that the focus of recent years by Peters, Naisbitt, Carlzon, and others has drawn our attention to catering to the customer or client in order to become a more excellent company. The customer benefits and the organization benefits. This is great, but the biblical expression of servant leadership is even more counter-cultural and even more profound. The person is the focus rather than the planned results. Also, the motivation and resources available from a relationship with God can produce change otherwise not possible by natural human effort. Becoming is more important than success.

The Bible seems to portray two types of servant leaders. One type represents those who start on the lower rung or are the weak of society like Esther, Rahab, David, Ruth, Timothy, and others. The more common are those who started out on the higher levels of society and were "forced into servant learning school" by God either through being sent to the wilderness, being thrown into prison or blinded. Moses, Joseph, Paul, the disciples, and others were men who had to change their course and experience what it meant to serve before they could lead in God's kingdom. Even Jesus spent time in the desert. I am sure we can think of people throughout history and in our own history who we would call servant leaders, because of their servant-first influence or the way they were raised up from low self esteem to impact others without the desire for recognition and success. Many passages in Scripture seem to indicate that the developmental process is that of servant-learning first, and then influence and leadership come through experience, maturity, and a desire to serve downward as well as upward.

There are leadership systems that have been handed down that inhibit one being able to serve because of man's need to succeed and be the best. Hierarchical systems that have a chief at the top encourage isolationism, competition, loneliness, and weakness at the top. Greenleaf suggests shared leadership, the first amongst equals, and I would like to add to that premise that group leadership needs to be at the bottom of the organizational chart so that the "first leader" is also the "chief servant" and helps facilitate the leadership of all others. The top then becomes subject to and a resource for the lower. Jesus knew how to do this within egalitarian and hierarchical groups by relating upward and downward. Everyone was a peer. I suggest that until we are able to treat everyone as upward, we cannot really treat everyone as a peer. Then we can respect a person's position because it is not a threat to us and the acceptance will help us communicate better with that person.

In egalitarian societies these concepts are not so radical, at least on the surface, but I contend that although ideal-sounding they can be of influence in any type of structural environment, and at any level, but will be the more profound, significant, and difficult in very authoritarian, strongly ethnocentric environments. I can think of a young African pastor, a Chinese biology teacher, a pilot in Peru, and many others who were changed inside out, and as a result tried some very radical things in their organizations with amazing results. They risked going against the cultural norms. They expected antagonism which eventually turned into positive results. The results were not the focus, the organization was not the focus, but their own desire to serve those with whom they worked and lived.

> *Greenleaf believes that institutions can serve and be served as well as individuals.*

In the following pages, we will study, discuss, and experiment to see how these concepts work out in a variety of cultural models that can be applied across cultures, times, and stratas with the realization that we can only get glimpses of how this works because of our human limitations.

Grace Preedy Barnes
Editor

Discovering "Servant" in Servant Leadership

by Kevin W. Mannoia

Summary: The term servant leadership is not so much a reference to a management style as it is a reference point to the identity of the leader.

Introduction

The first question I asked my class on Servant Leadership was, "Why are you here?" In one form or another, most of the students answered the question as one did: "I want to learn to do servant leadership, 'cause I heard it really works!" At face value, that response is more than a professor could want. Yet it gave me pause. I wondered, "Do they really know what they're in for? Where have they gotten the preconceived ideas they bring to the class?" As the days wore on, it became evident that they were like so many others who are caught in a pragmatic trap that filters everything through the grid of utility, one that gives top priority to results. In other words, if it works, it's good. If it doesn't, then it's not. Before long, I had to ask myself another question: "Why should I be skeptical about describing servant leadership as a management style that 'really works'?"

There is no doubt that we are seeing a substantial rise in interest in servant leadership both in the secular arena as well as the sacred. Leaders hear the ideas and are naturally drawn to the apparent selflessness of the paradigm that puts others first. This interest is reinforced by the results that servant leadership yields in real-life situations. Too many experiences of positive outcomes exist to deny that it has merit as a serious and increasingly attractive pattern of leadership.

> We are seeing a substantial rise in interest in servant leadership both in the secular arena as well as the sacred.

In the face of these results, then, the natural tendency is to approach servant leadership as a model or style. In launching on a journey to learn servant leadership, a person presumes he or she will be gaining skills in behaviors that will help others be fulfilled, and thereby fulfill the desires of the organization. The result is that the servant leader then will be effective. And isn't that the desire of every leader?

Kevin W. Mannoia, Ph.D., is Professor of Ministry and Chaplain to graduate programs and faculty at Azusa Pacific University. Having grown up in Brazil, he is a world Christian and has served in church leadership positions as a pastor, superintendent, bishop, as well as president of the National Association of Evangelicals, and most recently as Dean of Theology. His three books and various articles convey his priority to leadership formation and Kingdom principles.

But the genius of servant leadership is not really in its behaviors or in its outcomes. The result of learning servant leadership is not merely changed behavior – at least, it shouldn't be. Servant leadership is not so much a style of leadership as it is a condition of the leader. Its uniqueness is not in its outcomes but in its genesis. It is not a series of activities to be mimicked or skills to be acquired. Rather, it is a mindset, a life, an identity to be forged. Admittedly, there are behaviors that are descriptive of servant leaders, but they occur as a result of what the person has become. Anything less cheapens the depth and significance of servant leadership, which is a call first to be a servant. Because we always behave out of who we are, it is natural that a servant will exhibit servant leadership skills.

> *Servant leadership is not so much a style of leadership as it is a condition of the leader.*

Certainly, you can approach the subject as if it is a set of skills to be learned. Such skills may help in the practice of leadership. There is merit in recognizing that learned behavior, when repeated often, can become habitual. These habits can become second nature and begin to transform the character of a leader. This personal transformation happens from the outside in. But the true power of servant leadership is ultimately found in the inner being of the leader. It begins with identity questions that provide a solid foundation out of which skills will naturally flow with integrity and ultimate effectiveness through various styles of leadership. Therein lies the true genius of servant leadership.

The Model of a Leader

Identity gives rise to behavior. Who we are will always have an effect on what we do. Those are two dimensions of leadership and they are inseparable. They are like an iceberg. An iceberg has one tenth of its mass above the waterline. Nine tenths, then, lies beneath the waterline where no one can see it. The top of the iceberg represents the leadership activities that we perform – vision casting, managing, budgeting, decision-making, strategic planning, counseling, directing. The bottom of the iceberg represents the identity of the leader. It answers the question "Who am I?" while the top of the iceberg answers the question "What am I here to do?" Both are essential elements for a leader. But you can quickly see that one cannot exist without the other. The top of the iceberg is only able to keep balance and stability to the extent that the bottom is well formed and deep. The top represents performance while the bottom represents character. The top is doing, and the bottom is being.

A leadership style is merely the description of activities in the top of the iceberg and their effect on the surrounding context. Effectiveness in this pattern of thinking is defined by the results that come in tangible and measurable outcomes. If we think about leadership only in this dimension, we are assuming that outcomes or results are the priority and primary reference point for leadership.

In reality, wholeness and long-term effectiveness come from building integrity between who we are and what we do, between the bottom and the top of the iceberg. To relegate servant leadership only to the category of a leadership style limits it to the top of the iceberg which is only a fraction of who the leader really is. Furthermore, thinking of servant leadership as one method among many makes it entirely dependent upon the results of "doing" leadership. When servant leadership is seen first as the condition of the leader, then the priority is identity which will give rise to activity that is consistent with its nature. The bottom of the iceberg always provides a foundation and nature out of which activities in the top of the iceberg are performed. Servant leadership is much more than merely a style of leadership. It is a description of the leader himself or herself.

Putting the "servant" back in "servant leadership" means more than doing greater acts of service for others in fulfilling our leadership responsibility. It means shaping the character of the leader with identity questions that will transform the leader's very nature into that of a servant. The resulting activities of leadership, irrespective of the style of leadership used, will be servant motivated. Clearly, there are some activities that by nature are inconsistent with a servant identity. However, servant leadership may manifest itself in a diversity of behaviors that cross the standard lines of prescribed leadership styles. The foundation of servant leadership is the "bottom of the iceberg" identity of the leader which, when extended into "top of the iceberg" activities, shapes behaviors. It provides a level of discrimination that eliminates inconsistent actions and, at the same time, multiplies the effects of activities that are consistent with its nature.

Identity of a Servant

In reality, we all serve someone or something. The question is what or whom. It may be that upon careful examination, we find we are serving our own agenda. Self is probably the most prevalent master of a leader's life. In this paradigm, we strive to fulfill our own agendas. Self becomes the central point of reference for all activities. Personal betterment becomes the test against which all decisions are evaluated for effectiveness. The measure of good leadership, then, is whether we are in better shape and obtain greater power, prestige, or influence personally.

Another strong contender for center stage in a leader's life is others. At first the thought of serving other people sounds noble if not downright righteous. Yet at closer examination, it can be a pitfall for burnout and a frustrated vocation. Consider all the differing agendas of people in the organization. Trying to fulfill all of those while still maintaining some level of growth in the organization is a formula for overload. This is particularly true in volunteer organizations such as the church and is perhaps the greatest source of frustration for pastors. Their constant attempt to please people and serve them creates inner stresses that can quickly come to a breaking point in tough situations.

A third possibility as the primary objective in a leader's work is organizational performance. Outcomes or results overshadow all other agendas or interests. Leaders with this "master" may very quickly slide into a pattern of leadership that is controlling, manipulative, and potentially abusive to people unless there are careful checkpoints. They may be so intent upon seeing results that potential collateral damage in staff is inconsequential to them.

The healthiest, and perhaps only "master" of a true servant leader, is God. While this claim may sound general enough to be irrelevant, in reality it is the most relevant and healthiest point of reference for a leader to have. Clearly, there are many assumptions attached to such a declaration, but when understood well, the idea that servant leaders are first servants

> In reality, wholeness and long-term effectiveness come from building integrity between who we are and what we do.

of God helps a leader to find meaning, balance, fulfillment, and motivation in exercising various leadership activities in any context. Before you discard the idea as spiritual jargon, consider the reality that the uncontested greatest leader of all time was Jesus. In order to understand his effectiveness, we have to take a look behind the scene and get a glimpse of his identity. He did not come to set up an organization or to manipulate people into performance under his control. The best descriptor we have of him is that of a servant. But it's important to note that even though he was meeting the needs of people, he was not their servant. He came as a servant of God, the Father, and it was God's agenda that directed his activities. His service to people was to help them discover wholeness as they too came into an understanding of God's desire for them. Servant leaders do well to begin their journey of formation here.

> The healthiest, and perhaps only "master" of a true servant leader, is God.

The bottom of the iceberg, our identity, is the place where no one else sees. It is the ballast that gives our lives stability and meaning. Out of the overflow of that identity, our activities are motivated and focused not only in a manner consistent with the inner DNA of our being, but in a way that fulfills God's vocation and calling for us.

Making the willful choice to serve God means that first our nature is transformed. Our nature is affected by our submission to the one we serve. If the one we serve is self, we will by nature become selfish. If the ones we serve are others, we will become manipulative and insecure in the many different demands placed on us by others. If the one we serve is good and righteous, then we will become like minded. The character of the leader will take on the nature of the one he or she serves.

In addition to our nature being affected, our priorities are also affected based upon whom we serve. If we serve self, our priority is to preserve and exalt self at all cost. In serving God, however, we find that his priorities become ours. What is important to God becomes important to us. His greatest priority since creation has been to meet the needs of people. Hence, in serving God, our priorities become like his – to meet the needs of people thereby maximizing their sense of fulfillment and effectiveness. The difference, though, is that we do so not out of a manipulative motivation to achieve good results, but out of a deep desire to please the one we serve.

Serving God simply means trying to fulfill what God has in mind for us. That is the basis of vocation which has at its root a calling, a destiny, a deep passion and motivation that transcends the mere implementation of leadership activities. When a leader discovers this fountainhead, suddenly all of the activities in the top of the iceberg begin to make sense. They flow out of a natural wellspring of identity and are focused with consistency as the nature of that identity finds expression in actions. Who we are always gives rise to what we do. Our nature as a servant first will affect our actions as a leader.

The error that many students of leadership make is to assume that servant leadership is merely a style of leadership complete with formulas, behaviors, and patterns which, when learned well, will result in positive outcomes. Servant leadership is not merely a style. It is a condition of the leader. As such, a servant leader may employ a variety of leadership styles. What makes this leader a servant is the fact that he or she is acting out of servanthood to God, compelled by a God-given vocation in fulfilling a God-given destiny. It is most evident in the condition of the leader. So, while we may perform service for people, we are not their servants. A servant leader is servant to one.

Conclusion

In a day when efficiency and outcomes

are the center of attention for leaders and leadership studies, calling people to servant-hood is countercultural. It goes against the grain of a 21st century entrepreneurial, success-oriented culture. From the time we enter school until the day we enter the workforce, we are hammered with the importance of performance and results. The bottom line is the most influential element in promotions, hires, and bonuses. The expectation is that not much else is important as long as the results are good. Even the character of a person is minimized if performance is strong. And so, we create a culture that is built upon results, performance, and outcomes. While at first glance this appears to be effective, owing to the net improvement of organizations and their ability to service communities, it is a trap that can become destructive.

The shallow nature of performance-based identity leaves a leader dependent upon outcomes to determine personal value. If the outcomes of leadership activities are good, then the leader assumes she is a good person. Conversely, if performance is poor, the leader begins to think he is a bad person and begins to seek other, perhaps inappropriate, sources of personal validation. Burnout, moral failure, and misbehavior are all potential consequences of an identity that is based merely upon performance that fails. Arrogance, abuse, and self-centered corruption can become the consequences of performance-based identity that is successful. In either case, the value of a person is reduced to the ability to perform, and that individual becomes a commodity to be used or an asset to be leveraged.

Although the servant leadership model is best exemplified by the person of Jesus, it is a principle that applies universally to all people. It is not a style to be learned as much as it is a condition to be owned by the leader. For a leader the starting point is to ask the question, "Who am I?" As this leads to basic identity formation, the activities that follow in engaging the work situation will be shaped and adjusted into consistency. In that consistency, otherwise known as integrity, there is power and effectiveness that is healthy, productive, and selfless.

> *Our nature as a servant first will affect our actions as a leader.*

PERSONAL REFLECTION EXERCISE

INTRODUCTION FOR STUDENTS: You will discover as you study leadership that one of the major themes of Servant Leadership is personal reflection. Each article, therefore, is followed by two very different exercises. The first is a Personal Reflection Exercise that will always be based on what you have read.

They will also enhance your next exercise, the Small Group Learning Task. To get the most out of these important reflection exercises, do write as much as possible because it's in the uncovering of motives and experiences that you learn what your patterns in leadership have been and what personal motivations or challenges you will encounter in becoming a Servant Leader.

The following questions are adapted from material from the Robert K. Greenleaf Center.

YOUR AUTOBIOGRAPHY OF SERVING AND BEING SERVED

Your own story about how you have served and been served may reveal to you useful information for reflection. This worksheet can be used as an initial step in recalling your experiences serving and being served at different stages in your life.

CHILDHOOD EXPERIENCES WITH SERVICE

For starters, what are some of your first memories about being aware that someone else was doing something for you? Who were they, what did they do, and how did you feel as a result of being served?

What attitude about serving others was either spoken or demonstrated in your family or origin?

What are some early memories of consciously doing something on behalf of someone else? Recall as many details and feelings as possible.

ADULT EXPERIENCES WITH SERVICE

In your current employment or situation, what were some initial experiences of being served by someone else?

What do you recall now as the first helpful, serving thing you did for someone in your current situation?

SMALL GROUP LEARNING TASK

For maximum participation and learning, break up into small groups of no more than four.

Read Jerry Shaw's story and answer the questions that follow.

Jerry Shaw's Story

Jerry Shaw is a thirty-six-year-old single man who has be hired by the local Boys Club to design and manage after school programs for boys at risk. Seventy-three percent of the youth come from single parent homes. All are having some sort of trouble at school. Some of them are in trouble for breaking the law. Jerry comes from a Christian home with affirming parents. He really enjoyed going to school and wants to create and oversee the kinds of programs that will enable these at-risk boys to assimilate into their school and community. He has always wanted to work with troubled youth and although he has been a volunteer in church youth departments, he has yet to deal with boys at risk. He has heard about servant leadership and believes that it is the appropriate leadership model for him to follow in this new position.

1. According to this article, what is the starting point for Jerry if he wants to be a servant leader?

2. Let's say that the figure below represents an iceberg.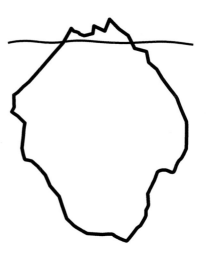

Using the example provided, draw your own iceberg on a blank sheet of paper. Inside the iceberg, below the line, name some inner qualities Jerry will need to draw on or develop if he is to be a servant leader at the Boys Club.

On the top of the iceburg (above the "water line"), list the job skills Jerry will also need if he is to be effective.

WHAT JERRY NEEDS TO BE EFFECTIVE AT WORK

JOB SKILLS

INNER QUALITIES

A Servant Leadership Definition and Model

by Jim Laub

Summary: If servant leadership is a viable paradigm for today's organizations, it is critical to define it and visualize how it operates in organizational life.

What is servant leadership? What does it look like in practice? How is servant leadership different from other mindsets of leadership? One of the challenges in leadership and servant leadership studies is that the concept has not been clearly defined in a way that it can be assessed and measured. If we are serious about servant leadership, we should be able to define it and provide a model of how it works in organizational life. Can we provide a model of servant leadership that allows an organization to determine if it, in fact, is operating in a servant-minded manner? This chapter will present a research-based definition and model of servant leadership that can set a foundation for understanding what servant leadership is and what it looks like when practiced.

Foundationally, servant leadership is a mindset. It is not a style of leadership to choose when addressing various situations; it is a foundational belief system about leadership, a distinct paradigm. It is a way of looking differently at those who are led, the role of the leader, and the purpose of leadership. Servant leaders are focused on the well being of those they lead. This is fundamental and essential. Other mindsets of leadership focus either on the leader or on the organization.

Servant leaders are concerned with the good of those they lead and believe firmly that this mindset will ultimately produce the greater good for the organization. Servant leaders do not put themselves first; they believe that the leader exists to serve those they lead. They know that leadership is not to promote the leader but to produce positive change in the world.

> Foundationally, servant leadership is a mindset.

The definition and model of servant leadership presented in this chapter were developed through a Delphi research process involving fourteen experts in the field of servant leadership. These experts were chosen based on the fact that they had written about servant leadership or had taught the subject at the university level.

Jim Laub Ed.D. is Dean of the MacArthur School of Continuing Education at Palm Beach Atlantic University where he is also Professor of Leadership Studies. He is president of the OLAgroup, creator of the Organizational Leadership Assessment (OLA) and author of several leadership training programs.

The expert panel included: Larry Spears, The Greenleaf Center for servant Leadership; Ann McGee-Cooper and Duane Trammell, Ann McGee-Cooper & Associates*; Jim Kouzes, Learning Systems, Inc.,/The Tom Peters Group; Dr. Bill Millard, Life Discovery and World Servants; Lea Williams, Bennett College; Dr. Joe Roberts, Suncoast Church of Christ; Jack Lowe, Jr., TD Industries; Dr. Pam Walker, Cerritos College; Grace Barnes, Azusa Pacific University; Ann Liprie-Spence, McMurray University; Deborah Campbell, Servant Leadership Community of West Ohio; Dr. Ted Ward, Trinity Evangelical Divinity School and Michigan State University; and Bishop Bennett Sims, The Institute for Servant Leadership.

> Servant leaders are concerned with the good of those they lead.

A three-round Delphi process was used. The first questionnaire provided a summary statement of the research purpose and goals, a brief description of the Delphi method being used, and forms for recording responses. The panel was asked to list at least ten characteristics of the servant leader. Once they completed the list, they were asked to open an envelope that contained a list of characteristics drawn from the literature. They then were asked to add to their list any of the characteristics from the literature listing they felt should be included. Along with this first questionnaire, a statement of assumptions was included to establish a framework for the Delphi question. This statement read:

This study is based on the assumption that there are characteristics of the servant leader which are observable within the context of organizational and team life. The characteristics of the servant leader may include behaviors, attitudes, values, and abilities.

The Delphi question itself read: What do you judge to be the characteristics of the servant leader? This first questionnaire produced sixty-seven distinct characteristics that then became the basis for the second part of the Delphi process.

The second questionnaire presented a compilation of all of the lists received from round one. This compiled list was provided with a semantic differential rating scale on which the experts were asked to rate each of the sixty-seven items. The scale included four values placed at regular intervals on a seven-point scale. The four values used are described below:

Essential: Without this characteristic, a person would not be a servant leader.

Necessary: This characteristic would normally be present in a person who is a servant leader.

Desirable: This characteristic is compatible with being a servant leader but is not really necessary.

Unnecessary: This characteristic probably has little or no relation to a person being a servant leader.

Experts were also asked to add additional characteristics that they felt needed to be added at this point. Three characteristics were added to the list for the next questionnaire for a cumulative total of seventy.

The third questionnaire included the results of the responses to round two. The results were presented using the same semantic scale as in round two with the median, twenty-fifth percentile, and seventy-fifth percentile of each characteristic rating marked. They were asked to rate each item once again, while providing their reasoning for any responses that fell outside of the middle 50 percent of the group response.

The median and inter-quartile range of total response for each item were computed to determine which characteristics were rated as "necessary" or "essential" for describing the servant leader. These characteristics then formed the basic constructs for the development of the servant leadership definition and model. A sign test was run on the inter-quartile ranges from rounds two and three to reveal a significant movement towards consensus by the expert panel. This movement towards consensus provides for a strong validation of the underlying constructs for the definition and model.

Definitions and Model

Servant Leadership is an understanding and practice of leadership that places the good of those led over the self-interest of the leader. Servant leadership promotes the valuing and development of people, the building of community, the practice of authenticity, the providing of leadership for the good of those led, and the sharing of power and status for the common good of each individual, the total organization, and those served by the organization.

The Servant Organization is an organization in which the characteristics of servant leadership are displayed through the organizational culture and are valued and practiced by the leadership and workforce.

Display Authenticity

Servant leadership begins with a different view of yourself as leader. You are to be open, real, approachable, and accountable to others. You are not higher than others due to your "position." In fact, position speaks to responsibility not value. As you work with people within organizations, you will serve them if you display the qualities of authenticity.

Open and Accountable

Resist the tendency to protect yourself at all costs. When you make mistakes, admit them. Recognize that you are accountable to others and not just those who are "over"

you. A servant has nothing to prove and can fully risk being open with others.

Willing to Learn

Come to other people in the role of a learner. As a servant you know that you have much to learn and each person can be your teacher. You don't always know what is needed and what to do. You are willing to listen before making suggestions. You ask a lot of questions, and you are sincerely interested in the answers.

Honesty and Integrity

You refuse to cut corners on the truth. When you make a promise, you do everything you can to fulfill it. People learn that they can trust what you say and that your actions fit your words. You are ethical in how you treat people and act within situations.

Value People

Servant leadership requires a different view of others. People are to be valued and developed, not used for the purposes of the leader. As a leader I accept the fact that people have present value, not just future potential. People seem to have an innate ability to know whether or not they are being valued, whether or not they are trusted. As a servant we accept a person's value up front. We give them the gift of trust without requiring that they earn it first. As you work with people in organizations, you will serve them if you display the qualities of valuing people.

> *Servant leadership promotes the valuing and development of people.*

Serve Others First

Put others before yourself. Focus on their needs and how you can best meet them. Don't fall to the temptation that the role of the leader must be protected at all costs. Serve others before your own self-interest.

Believe and Trust in People

Give others your trust. Believe that they can do the job. Envision their potential. Look beyond the immediate externals to find the true value of another. When you trust people, they will react positively to that trust and will become more trustworthy.

Listen Receptively

When we truly listen to another, we will hear him or her if we listen non-judgmentally. We listen to learn, to understand. We listen because we know that it is one of the best ways to show that we value another.

Develop People

As servants we view others differently. Part of my responsibility is to help others to grow towards their potential as servants and leaders. Therefore, I am looking to create a dynamic learning environment that encourages growth and development. As I interact with others, I am conscious of what we are learning together. The mistakes of others are opportunities to learn. We know that people have both present value and future potential. As leaders, we are part of helping them to realize that potential. As you work with people within organizations, you will serve them if you display the qualities of developing people.

> A servant has nothing to prove and can fully risk being open with others.

Provide for Learning

Offer people opportunities for new learning. Provide an atmosphere where mistakes can lead to new insights. Join them in learning. Don't expect to always be right. Realize that failure brings learning that success never can.

Model appropriate Behavior

Don't just tell others what to do. Model it for them and do it with them. We help people to develop by working alongside them so that they are able to learn from us—and with us.

Build Up Through Affirmation

Encourage others; honor others; accept others; build up others. Catch others doing it right. Recognize accomplishments and celebrate creativity. Use words; let them hear you say words of encouragement. Be intentional with your affirmation.

Build Community

Servant leaders have a different way of looking at how people work together. They desire to build community and a sense that we are part of a loving, caring team with a shared goal to accomplish. We resist the tendency to "just get the job done." We are just as concerned with the relationships of the people doing the job. We know that people are more impacted by the quality of relationships than they are by the accomplishment of tasks. Therefore, we will work intentionally to build a community that works together and learns to serve one another in the process. As you work with people within organizations, you will serve them if you display the qualities of building community.

Build Relationships

People need the time and space to be together—to share, to listen, to reflect. They need to get to know one another. Don't encourage lone-ranger success over team accomplishment. Encourage friendships to emerge.

Work Collaboratively

Don't allow the natural competitiveness between different individuals to characterize the atmosphere of the group. We don't want to "win" at the expense of the team.

Work alongside the other leaders to model this kind of work.

Value Differences

Respect and celebrate differences in ethnicity, gender, age, and culture. Be aware of your own prejudices and biases. Confront them so that no individual or group feels less valued by your dealings with them. We enhance our group by welcoming the various contributions of others. Resist sameness and compliance. Value and celebrate differences.

Provide Leadership

A servant leader leads, for the good of those being led. Leadership involves vision, action, mobilization, and change. The servant will not neglect to take appropriate action; in fact, leaders have a bias for action. This initiative-taking comes not from being driven to personal ambition but by being called to serve the highest needs of others.

Envision the Future

Leadership is future oriented. The leader looks ahead to envision what could be, and should be. Servant leaders recognize that they serve as partners with other leaders who also are looking ahead to the future. Servant leaders share their vision openly with the goal of creating a new shared vision with others.

Take Initiative

Leadership takes action. It doesn't hold back in order to protect the leader from making mistakes. The servant leader moves out in order to serve others—and to serve the consensus mission of the group.

Clarify Goals

Leadership is clear on where it is going. The servant leader uses open communication to point the direction that the group is committed to pursue. The leader encourages accountability to the predetermined goals—for themselves and for others.

Share Leadership

Every leader has power and must continually make choices as to how that power will be used. Power is the ability to act. Servant leaders share the power they have with others so that others can lead, thus increasing the potential influence and impact of leadership.

Share the Vision

The vision of a group does not belong to a single leader. A clear vision of the future shared by the entire group becomes a powerful magnet drawing together all of the resources, skills, and abilities of the team. Vision comes to leaders who see, and a shared vision occurs when our individual vision aligns toward an agreed upon future.

Share the Power

Power is the ability to do, the ability to act. In organizational terms it becomes the ability to make important decisions, allocate resources, and move forward to make things happen. Shared leadership empowers all people

> As a leader I accept the fact that people have present value, not just future potential.

to act, for the good of the group and the mission of the organization.

Share the Status

Leadership is not position, status, or prestige. Servant leaders resist the strong tendency to accept the special perks and privileges of a leadership position. They know that all people need to be affirmed and recognized for their inherent value and for what they contribute to the success of the team.

What are the implications of this definition and model of servant leadership? How might it be used? There is an individual application as each leader could consider these characteristics in a self-assessment of their own leadership. There are limitations to this, of course, as leaders are not always the best at accurately assessing how their leadership practice affects others. Another application of this model is to use it to assess servant leadership within organizations.

The term "servant organization" is not found in the literature, though Robert Greenleaf spoke of the institution as servant. Greenleaf, however, addressed the organizational issues involved rather than the idea of assessing an organization in light of the characteristics of servant leadership. This author believes that the servant organization is a natural extension and application of the concept of servant leadership. Leaders do not operate in a vacuum; they operate within organizational structures which include managers, workers, vendors, and customers. The characteristics of the servant leader may be applied to an entire organization, or a workgroup within an organization, as well as an individual leader. Organizations have a significant impact on the people they employ, on the customers they serve, and on the society at large. This impact goes be-

> *Realize that failure brings learning that success never can.*

yond one leader or a group of leaders. Servant leadership should become characteristic of the organizational culture in order to produce the most benefit.

In light of this, the Organizational Leadership Assessment (OLA) was developed to take this definition and model of leadership and use it to assess the presence of servant leadership within organizations. The OLA is a 66-item assessment instrument that is designed to be taken by people at all levels of the organization—its leaders, managers, and workforce—to assess the level of servant leadership present within the organization. This kind of assessment is useful for developing servant leadership within organizations as well as conducting research on this critical topic.

This definition and model are offered as a means to understand a topic that is too often vague and personally defined. Servant leadership as a concept needs to be clearly understood, assessed, and developed. It needs to be researched and, therefore, must become operational and observable. On a personal level, we must be able to determine if we are truly servant leaders in order to make the kind of impact for change that only a servant leadership mindset can provide.

NOTES

*Panel members Ann McGee-Cooper and Duane Trammell worked together on a single response for each part of the survey and are therefore counted as one respondent.

PERSONAL REFLECTION EXERCISE

In our post-modern world, we tend to have ambivalent feelings about organizations. We know we need them, but we are not always comfortable with the impersonal climate and structure they represent. Dream a little. Suppose you were the CEO of an organization. Describe the corporation or ministry you would want to create. Include in your description any personal or job skills you would need to be an effective CEO of this organization.

SMALL GROUP LEARNING TASKS

1. In small groups of no more than four, identify a time when you felt you truly belonged in an organization. (Church, school, corporation…) Describe the impact this had upon you.

2. Read the following scenarios. Using the characteristics on pages 11–13 of this article, name the ones appropriate for the attention of the senior servant leader in this situation. Also analyze what might be done to correct this situation.

Bill is trying valiantly to keep up with his work load, but his wife has just been diagnosed with cancer. Not only is he distracted, he's having to take a lot of time off to accommodate her needs.

Tristin has just been hired to be a key player in the research and development team at a high tech company. She has been assured that at this corporation all employees are treated with equality. As she drives into the parking lot her first day at work, she notices that the parking spaces closest to the front door are designated for the highest salaried, top executive positions in the company.

Brian sees a pattern surfacing in his meetings with Tom who comes to the meetings with an attitude that there's going to be a fight. Yesterday he came to the meeting and slammed papers on the table. He sighed deeply when Brian spoke. He shuffled through papers and read when others were speaking.

Choosing a Leadership Model:

Servant Leadership at a Glance

by Markus Melliger

Summary: Although there are a number of contemporary leadership models, there is one philosophy that has a two thousand-year history behind it.

Whether we are in an "official" or "unofficial" leadership position, we all have our individual leadership philosophies. Whether consciously or not, we hold to some strategy by which we lead others. In the following article, I would like to explore some of these philosophies and then point us in the direction of the model of servant leadership.

Some Leadership Philosophies

The following list gives us an idea of some commonly held leadership philosophies:

The "King or Queen." Someone who subscribes to this leadership model sees his or her leadership position as an inalienable right, one inherited by birth, through family or descent. The King or Queen sees his or her position as one given by God or a higher power and, naturally, one that cannot be taken away. Once the King is on the throne, you know he or she intends to stay!

The "Colonialist." The one who subscribes to this leadership philosophy views his or her race and culture as superior to others. Therefore, by principle, the Colonialist's own way of life, culture, language, and leadership decisions are superior and cannot legitimately be put into question by people from other cultures and races. While the Colonialist may feel great about himself or herself, unfortunately, others don't!

The "Dictator." He or she has taken a leadership position by force. It will be defended by force, it is beyond dispute, and it is not open for discussion. The Dictator is always right because he or she has surrounded himself exclusively by yes-men—or yes-women! But it's only a matter of time before such a leader falls.

The "General." He or she leads by commands that cannot be disobeyed. Generals view people as a commodity that can and should be spent for the achievement of a higher goal to which they feel they have a mandate. No matter what the human cost, Generals tend to feel they are above accountability.

> *Whether consciously or not, we hold to some strategy by which we lead others.*

Markus Melliger holds a master's degree in social science (leadership studies) from Azusa Pacific University. He has worked as Bible translator in Papua New Guinea since 1992.

The *"Politician."* He or she tries to please a majority as a means to get elected or re-elected. Because the Politician is dependent on the approval of a majority, he or she makes promises that often cannot be kept; when opinions change, the Politician shifts positions to please the majority again. There is always a segment among the followership that feel cheated and lied to, an accusation to which the Politician seems oblivious. When the Politician then does not get re-elected, he or she is surprised.

The *"Patron or Patroness."* Such leaders are quite convinced of themselves as the providers of what is "best" for others. They may feel a great sense of duty and responsibility for others and may be successful to some degree, but they tend to treat adults as children and keep them

> *"Servant leadership" as a leadership philosophy was first formulated by Robert K. Greenleaf in the middle of the twentieth century.*

that way. Adults, however, resent being treated as children.

The *"Expert."* He or she always knows more than others. While Experts may be open for correction, their vast knowledge tends to threaten people and serves as a barrier between them and those they lead. As long as the Expert is not willing to learn from non-experts, open dialogue is impossible. And as long as the Expert sees himself or herself as "the expert," professional pride is rampant.

The *"Priest or Priestess."* Such leaders feel they are the representatives of a higher power and see themselves as the vital link between that higher power and people. They often have a word from a higher authority that others don't have. Because of that claim, they tend to yield power over people, a power which, because of its source, appears to be beyond dispute. Priests and Priestesses tend to create a dependency on people, withholding information from them, and they can easily

lead by decree and manipulation. In the long run, however, people resent being manipulated.

What other leadership philosophies come to mind? It is quite possible that there are numerous other leadership models that we follow. I listed the ones above to remind us which of the philosophies we tend to apply most often, although we may use a combination of several. However, there is a leadership philosophy that, I think, is vastly superior to all the ones listed above. It is called "servant leadership."

Servant Leadership

In contrast to the leadership philosophies illustrated above, servant leadership is a strategy that puts others first and seeks leadership by means of serving others.

"Servant leadership" as a leadership philosophy was first formulated by Robert K. Greenleaf in the middle of the twentieth century. Greenleaf had spent most of his adult life in the professional world, working for one of the largest companies in the U.S. Towards retirement he started publishing essays and presenting speeches. In the seventies he published a collection of his articles in a book called, *Servant Leadership – A Journey into the Nature of Legitimate Power and Greatness.*

Greenleaf coined the term "servant leader," which at first glance seems to be a contradiction in terms. Leaders, according to Greenleaf, are to be servants of others, servants of society, whether they are leaders of institutions, schools, churches or foundations, or serve as trustees. When leaders learn to "serve" their organizations, he stressed, society will ultimately change for its own good.

In his first essay, The Servant as Leader, Greenleaf wrote, "It begins with the natural feeling that one wants to serve, to serve first. Then conscious choice brings one to aspire to lead. The difference manifests itself in the care taken by the servant – first to make sure that other people's highest-priority needs are being served. The best test is: Do those served grow as persons; do they, while being served become healthier, wiser, freer, more autonomous, more likely themselves to become servants?" (Spears, p. 4).

Servant leadership, as I understand it, is not a theory that's fully developed down to the last detail, and I think that is a good thing. Its open-endedness, I think, requires a leap that brings us closer to the one who is the supreme model of servant leadership. While Greenleaf is credited with creating the term "servant leader," the concept, of course, goes back to Jesus Christ who two thousand years ago modeled for us true servant leadership. The following two passages from the Gospels illustrate very well that Jesus is the true creator, both in word and deed, of the concept of servant leadership:

"So Jesus called them together and said, 'You know that in this world kings are tyrants, and officials lord it over the people beneath them. But among you it should be quite different. Whoever wants to be a leader among you must be your servant, and whoever wants to be first must be the slave of all. For even I, the Son of Man, came here not to be served but to serve others, and to give my life as a ransom for many" (Mark 10:42-45).[1]

"You call me 'Teacher' and 'Lord,' and you are right, because it is true. And since I, the Lord and Teacher, have washed your feet, you ought to wash each other's feet. I have given you an example to follow. Do as I have done to you" (John 13:13-15).

The call for us is to "translate" these familiar passages into everyday situations when we are confronted with leadership challenges, whether those challenges relate to family life, encounters with co-workers or ministry to others.

What are some leadership challenges you are facing right now?

How can you see the principle of servant leadership in these passages?

How can you meaningfully and effectively apply these passages in your leadership challenges?

Servant Leadership Applied

As noted earlier, the model of servant leadership is not a leadership philosophy that has been theoretically analyzed down to the last detail. Rather, it is to be "fleshed out" on a day-to-day basis in the community of others. From my reading on this subject and conversations with colleagues, I have listed characteristics that I think capture the essence of servant leadership.

A servant leader...
- puts others first
- builds others up
- is committed to the growth of people
- encourages people
- empowers people
- is a listener
- facilitates dialogue
- develops genuine empathy
- builds community
- works for the good of society
- keeps the well-being of others in mind
- admits mistakes
- is a faithful steward
- leads by example

This list is obviously not exhaustive and is deliberatively left open-ended.

Some further insights can be gleaned from the following list of characteristics comparing a "boss" with a "leader." The author of the list, Harry Gordon Selfridge, was the developer of one of the largest department stores in London.[2] Selfridge came up with his understanding of leadership at the beginning of the twentieth

> A servant leader is committed to the growth of people.

century, and although he doesn't use the term "servant leader," the principle can be clearly seen in the role of the "leader."

Similarly, Pat MacMillan does not usually use the term "servant leadership" in his book, *The Performance Factor: Unlocking the Secrets of Teamwork*. But his comparison of a traditional leadership style with the leadership style of a team leader in today's world is enlightening. The principle of servant leadership is apparent in the role team leaders play (p. 103).

In what other ways can the principles of servant leadership be applied in today's world?

Conclusion

MacMillan provides an insightful summary regarding the essence of servant leadership (p. 99):

"Although this principle is ageless, in practice it is quite rare. Servant leadership is much more an attitude than a skill. Service and empowerment are inextricably linked. If the team members don't feel served, they will stop empowering (and accepting) the leader. If the leader doesn't feel empowered, it's quite likely that he or she will stop serving. Authoritative and controlling leaders are often insecure people attempting to take what they have not been given. Because they were not given acceptance (however they define it), they demand it. The key to becoming a servant leader is to see leadership as a role from which to serve, not a position to be served."

In my view, the principle of servant leadership is vastly superior to all other leadership philosophies. A true servant leader can mean the difference in the future of any organization.

The Boss...	*The Leader...*
drives people	coaches people
depends upon authority	depends on good will
says "I"	says "We"
fixes the blame for the breakdown	fixes the breakdown
knows how it is done	shows how it is done
says "Go!"	says "Let's go!"

Traditional Leaders...	*Team Leaders...*
manage	lead
tell	listen
direct	ask questions
convince	discuss
decide/provide answers	facilitate
control	coach
supervise	release initiative and creativity in others

PERSONAL REFLECTION EXERCISE

1. Review the commonly held leadership styles on pp. 17-18 of this article. Consider a boss you have had who fits into one of those categories. Write about any negative impact that leadership style had upon you.

2. Now suppose the roles were reversed and you were suddenly the boss in this situation. What would you do differently? Include how you might expect these changes to impact the employees influenced by it.

SMALL GROUP LEARNING TASK

Form small groups of no more than four. Read the facts about geese. For each fact, identify at least one servant leadership lesson. Using a Sunshine Wheel, write GEESE LESSONS in the center and write your lessons on the spokes.

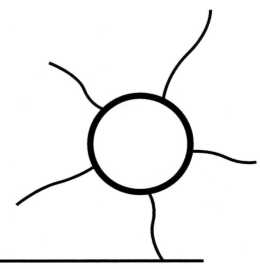

When you are finished, post your Sunshine Wheel for others to review and compare to their own leadership lessons discovered. Appoint a spokesperson for your group. We'll have a gallery walk to discover the lessons we have learned from the geese.

Fact 1: As each goose flaps its wings, it creates an "uplift" for the birds that follow. By flying in a "B" formation, the whole flock adds 71 percent greater flying range than if each bird flew alone.

Lesson:

Fact 2: When a goose falls out of formation, it suddenly feels the drag and resistance of flying alone. It quickly moves back into formation to take advantage of the lifting power of the bird immediately in front of it.

Lesson:

Fact 3: When the lead goose tires, it rotates back into the formation and another goose flies to the point position.

Lesson:

Fact 4: The geese flying in formation honk to encourage those up front to keep up their speed.

Lesson:

Fact 5: When a goose gets sick, wounded or shot down, two geese drop out of formation and follow it down to help it and protect it. They stay with it until it dies or is able to fly again. Then, they launch out with another formation or catch up with the flock.

Lesson:

SUMMARY OF SERVANT LEADERSHIP LESSONS FROM GEESE

REFERENCES

Covey, Stephen R. 1990. *The Seven Habits of Highly Effective People – Powerful Lessons in Personal Change.* New York: Simon & Schuster.

DePree, Max. 1989. *Leadership Is an Art.* New York: Dell.

Greenleaf, Robert K. 1977. *Servant Leadership – A Journey into the Nature of Legitimate Power and Greatness.* New York: Paulist Press.

MacMillan, Pat. 2001. *The Performance Factor – Unlocking the Secrets of Teamwork.* Nashville, Tennessee: Broadman and Holman Publishers.

Maxwell, John C. 1989, 94. *Be a People Person: Effective Leadership Through Effective Relationships.* Colorado Springs: Chariot Victor Publishing.

Miller, Calvin. 1995. *The Empowered Leader – 10 Keys to Servant Leadership.* Nashville, Tennessee: Broadman & Holman Publishers.

Spears, Larry C., ed. 1995. *Reflections on Leadership – How Robert K. Greenleaf's Theory of servant Leadership Influenced Today's Top Management Thinkers.* New York: John Wiley & Sons, Inc.

NOTES

[1] Scripture quotations are taken from the *Holy Bible, New Living Translation*, copyright 1996. Used by permission of Tyndale House Publishers, Inc., Wheaton Illinois 60189. All rights reserved.

[2] Mentioned in John C. Maxwell, *Be a People Person: Effective Leadership Through Effective Relationships*, pp. 77f.

Empowering People for Leadership

by Grace Preedy Barnes

Summary: The practice of empowerment as stewardship places information, resources, and power in the hands of those who are closest to the ones being helped or served.

Introduction

Christmas night my husband, Doug, and I returned from a wonderful day away with relatives. As we both settled down to a quiet evening together, I decided to read in the living room and turned on the stereo and lit the fireplace. I put on the Three Tenors tape, which I had just received as a gift, and allowed my mind to wander.

> The challenge of leadership is to know the needs and readiness of the follower.

Earlier that fall I had been asked to teach three new-to-me courses for the spring semester at Azusa Pacific University, and so I knew that I had a lot of reading and planning to do. The encouragement to "throw out the old course outlines" and start afresh, if I wished, released me to think creatively late into the night. I not only felt energized by the environment but also freed to explore new ways of teaching and designing courses that would motivate students to learn and grow. As a professor I always look at a new semester as a fresh start, a clean slate, which utilizes the past but creates something new that builds towards the future. I remember expressing to Doug, "What an empowering evening this has been!"

The Purpose and Nature of Empowerment

The term "empowerment" is popular today because in many ways it signifies the antithesis of old forms of power that were often tied to control, force, wealth, and violence. Even knowledge has been used as a power to condemn and separate people in ways that become violent, restrictive, and controlling. This kind of power destroys rather than builds; it seizes rather than frees. But empowerment is the process whereby power is transferred and released from one person to another. It is the giving of power, rather than the acquiring of it, and it allows one person to get involved with another in order to remove distance and barriers.

Empowerment, however, is not just a handing off or delegating process. This too can be damaging if a person is not ready to

Grace Preedy Barnes, Ph.D., is Professor of Organizational Leadership and program director of The Operation Impact at Azusa Pacific University which offers the MAOL degree program worldwide. She has taught in more than 25 countries and traveled to many more along with the 50+ faculty who travel to teach up to 600 students per year.

be left on his or her own. The challenge of leadership is to know the needs and readiness of the follower. It is a balancing act of challenge and support. I, as a person, am empowered when power that I do not have is released to me, not in a constricted, manipulative type of control that results in dependence or conformity, but in a way that allows me to express my God-given gifts and personhood. As Parker Palmer states in his address "Remembering the Heart of Higher Education," "We must understand that the best leaders are those who evoke not the fears of other people but their gifts" (2).

Jesus engaged in empowerment when he set people free to follow, to serve, and to give themselves away. He did the unthinkable, the politically incorrect, the unkosher, the impolite by empowering such people as the adulteress, the tax collector, the leper, and many other "scum bags" of the day.

Empowerment says, "Yes, you can, and you may" and "I trust you." As an empowerer I let go and release control of the other person, the outcome, the way things take place, and even the process. Empowerment is a giving of power that also provides for underpinning and support. Jesus said, "I am with you always" (Matthew 28:20). The role of the Holy Spirit is that of guide and supporter, not controller or director (John 16:13).

The Process of Empowerment

In the process of divine empowerment, we become partners with God, empowered to accomplish his work, to follow, and lead at the same time, to be servant leaders. The discipline of obeying, following, and serving God ironically leads to the development of leadership that serves and energizes others. The more we obey and serve God, the more we are given responsibility to become stewards who nurture, enhance, and allow

for growth and development in others. Max DuPree (9, 11) suggests that

"it is fundamental that leaders endorse a concept of persons. This begins with an understanding of the diversity of people's gifts and talents and skills.

"Understanding and accepting diversity enables us to see that each of us is needed. It also enables us to begin to think about being abandoned to the strengths of others. Of admitting that we cannot know or do everything...

"The first responsibility of a leader is to define reality. The last is to say thank you. In between the two, the leader must become a servant and a debtor. That sums up the progress of an artful leader."

Who this is the servant leader? According to Robert K. Greenleaf (7),

"the servant leader is servant first... It begins with the natural feeling that one wants to serve, to serve first. Then conscious choice brings one to aspire to lead... The difference manifests itself in the care taken by the servant—first to make sure that other people's highest priority needs are being served. The best test, difficult to administer, is: do those served grow as persons; do they, while being served, become healthier, wise, freer, more autonomous, more likely themselves to become servants? And what is the effect on the least privileged in society? Will they benefit, or at least, not be further deprived?"

"Go ye into all the world and empower" (Matthew 28:19)—this is the force of Jesus' commission to "make disciples" in a ministry of baptizing and teaching

> Jesus engaged in empowerment when he set people free to follow, to serve, and to give themselves away.

that leaves people empowered and changed from the encounter. Often in carrying out this commission we reduce it to formulas guaranteeing specific outcomes rather than allowing it to release people to both be and do in discovery of their giftedness. Parker Palmer in his book The Active Life *explores the paradox of action and contemplation and identifies the difference between instrumental and expressive action (23):*

"The instrumental image, which dominates Western culture, portrays action as a means to predetermined ends, as an instrument or tool of our intentions. The only possible measure of such action is whether it achieves the ends at which it is aimed. Instrumental action is governed by the logic of success and failure; it discourages us from risk-taking because it values success over learning, and it abhors failure whether we learn from it or not… Only when we act expressively do we move toward full aliveness and authentic power. An expressive act is one that I take not to achieve a goal outside myself but to express a conviction, a leading, a truth that is within me. An expressive act is often taken because if I did not take it I would be denying my own insight, my gift, my nature. By taking an expressive act, an act not obsessed with outcomes, I come closer to making the contribution that is mine to make in the scheme of things."

> **Empowerment is a giving of power that also provides for underpinning and support.**

One of the leadership questions becomes, how do we achieve goals and objectives for ourselves or for an organization and yet allow people to develop and contribute according to who God wants them to be and do? Graeme Irvine, former president of World Vision International, has put it this way(2):

" 'Empowerment' can occur when people discover within themselves, their community and their context, the resources needed to bring about positive change, and begin to exercise control over their own destiny. This is good. As Christians, we believe this empowerment comes primarily through faith in Jesus Christ and commitment to the values of the kingdom of God he proclaimed.

"But power is seductive. It is prone to abuse in order to get one's own way, protect one's own position or advance one's own cause. It offers an illusion of security or influence.

The ones who have power, then, are the ones to give it away. Those who do not have it must be given it in order that they might enter the dialogue or come to the table. Empowering them becomes a great act of love because of the realization that the person being empowered may make serious mistakes with that power and the mistakes may even be costly to the individual who is empowering. Christ suffered a great deal of abuse because of those he chose to free from bondage and allowed to participate with him (Romans 15:3).

The practice of empowerment as stewardship places information, resources, and power in the hands of those who are closest to the ones who are being helped or served. From an organizational perspective, it means, according to Peter Block in his book *Stewardship: Choosing Service over Self Interest,* that our expectations of people in power must change. It means holding in trust the well-being of the larger entity—the organization, the community, or the earth. Service becomes more important than control. There is pride in leadership but humility in stewardship. Entitlement becomes empowerment run amuck!

The Practice of Empowerment

Leadership today is vulnerable. In fact, it is wobbly. Historically, leadership studies focused on the influence of "great men" who had bigger-than-life influence on people and history. Later it was determined that certain traits were important. Since then, studies have led to a very complex view of leadership that is contingent on interactions between the leader, the follower, and the situation. The readiness of the follower, the complexities of the situation, and the interaction between the person, the position, and the process are all important to the nature of leadership. The definitions of leadership have broadened. Leadership is fragile today because we are not sure what is needed. A study at Fuller Theological Seminary conducted by J. Robert Clinton has shown that very few leaders finish well.

Because of the speed of change today, with urbanization, globalization, computerization, feminization, values confusion, and many other factors, we are having to look at new ways to view and develop leadership. The church's bottom-line imperative is to unlock the laity so that it can achieve its fullest capacity. The rise of the seven-day-a-week church indicates that the role of leadership is spreading throughout the church rather than being focused on one individual pastor. Jesus said, "The greatest among you will be your servant; for whoever exalts himself will be humbled and whoever humbles himself will be exalted" (Matthew 23:11-12).

One of the other findings in Clinton's study at Fuller Theological Seminary was that significant relationships were very important to finishing well. Older styles of leadership often did not allow for nurture and the role of mentors, personal boards of directors, and systems of support that provide health and wholeness for individuals and institutions.

Paul the Apostle seems to have practiced this approach to leadership development and church planting. His life and ministry demonstrated the incarnation of servant leadership ideas in the way he selected and trained leaders and established churches. Paul saw himself as a servant of Christ and a steward. He encouraged people to serve Christ and others, and encouraged leadership development according to a person's giftedness rather than one's position or title (Ephesians 4:11-16; emphasis added):

"And his [Christ's] gifts were that some should be apostles, some prophets, some evangelists, some pastors and teachers, for the equipment of the saints, for the work of the ministry, for building up the body of Christ, until we all attain to the unity of the faith and of the knowledge of the Son of God, to mature manhood, to the measure of the stature of the fullness of Christ; so that we may no longer be children, tossed to and fro and carried about with every wind of doctrine, by the cunning of men, by their craftiness in deceitful wiles. Rather, speaking the truth in love, we are to grow up in every way into him, who is the head, unto Christ, from whom the whole body, joined and knit together by every joint with which it is supplied, when each part is working properly, makes bodily growth and upbuilds itself in love."

> The first responsibility of a leader is to define reality.—Max DuPree

There are so many needs to be principle-centered with its focus on character and holiness rather than on personality and power. Education and training should provide principles that guide, participation that encourages ownership rather than entitlement, and leadership that is more organic than mechanical. Organic leadership is concerned with understanding the whole, relationships, and processes. Leaders are gardeners and cultivators and are trying to encourage an environment that produces interdependence and energy. Leaders become facilitators and coordinators, mentors and servants.

As I reflect on the impact of these concepts on my own life, I can recall mentors who have empowered me as well as students who have dared to make radical changes in their own leadership styles and organizational structures. Many times these changes were jeered at or discouraged, but through perseverance dramatic changes took place that resulted in the empowerment of others!

Empowerment leads to…
- Release
- Freedom
- Personal Expression
- Development
- Growth
- Energy
- Aliveness
- Wholeness
- Creativity
- Reproduction

PERSONAL REFLECTION EXERCISE

Consider a time in your leadership experience when you were empowered to lead effectively. Write about the factors that enabled that empowerment. What were the skills you learned and used? What was the impact of your empowering upon the people and the work you were leading?

Small Group Learning Task

1. In small groups of three or four, create two charts. First a T chart of needs. Name the 10 greatest needs in the world today and the 10 specific needs you see in the people you lead and serve. Then create a chart of your conclusions about empowering leaders to meet those needs. (Use any format you like for this chart.) Post your charts alongside each other on the wall. We will see and hear your ideas.

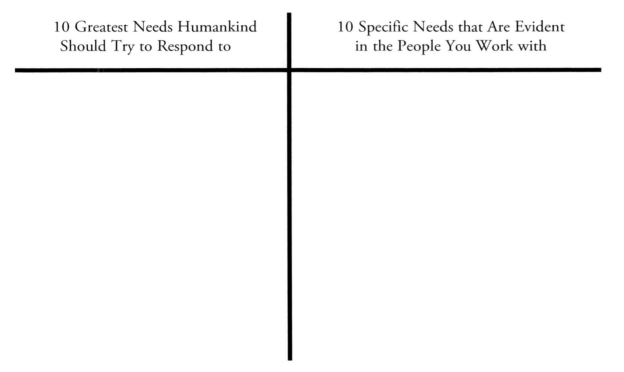

10 Greatest Needs Humankind Should Try to Respond to	10 Specific Needs that Are Evident in the People You Work with

Our Conclusions About Empowering Leaders to Meet These Needs:

REFERENCES

Block, Peter, *Stewardship: Choosing Service Over Self Interest.* San Francisco, CA: Berrett-Koehler, 1993.

Clinton, J. Robert. *The Making of a Leader.* Colorado Springs, CO: NavPress, 1988.

DuPree, Max. *Leadership Is an Art.* New York, NY: Dell, 1989.

Greenleaf, Robert K. *The Servant as Leader.* Diamond Bar, CA: Robert K. Greenleaf Center, 1991.

Irvine, Graeme. "The Illusion of Power," in *Together* (World Vision International, Monrovia, CA) (January-March, 1992): 2.

Palmer, Parker J. *The Active Life.* San Francisco, CA: Harper & Row, 1991.

Palmer, Parker J. "Remembering the Heart of Higher Education." Keynote address, AAHE National Conference on Higher Education, 1993.

The Triangular Dimension of Servant Leadership

by Christine Wood

Summary: The three-fold nature of servant leadership can be best illustrated by a triangular illustration representing functional leadership, relational leadership, and contextual leadership.

A leader is a person who develops a broad range of skills that equip him or her to walk alongside another and move them through the process of becoming "healthier, wiser, freer, more autonomous and more of a servant."[1]

Servant leadership is not for sissies. It requires a serious and courageous delving into one's own life. It means facing inadequacy and weakness effectively so that we might better serve others when they must face the issues that hold them back from becoming more functional human beings. It also means that we own our strengths to the extent that we will refine and offer them in service to others.

We're all products of individualism, pluralism, a deluge of information, and personal disappointment. Ours is a society of people who demand a voice, instant relief, and quick solutions. Clearly, we are living with problems we need to tackle. This is not the time to wring our hands or throw in the towel. This is not the time to rush out and initiate change for "change sake." This is not the time to put more energy into methods of leadership that have not proven effective. It is the time to create a comprehensive leadership style that can move us through the complex issues of tackling tough problems. To get beneath the problems, individual propensities, and the clamor of life in this emerging century, servant leadership offers us a model from which we can launch useful and practical solutions to the challenges before us.

> *We're all products of individualism, pluralism, a deluge of information, and personal disappointment.*

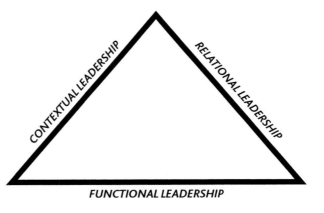

Christine Wood, MA in Organizational Leadership, is an author, consultant, and educator. She is an adjunct professor in leadership studies at Azusa Pacific University where she teaches both nationally and internationally. She is currently engaged in developing leadership curriculums, Bible studies and outreach programs for Christian organizations.

Larry Spears, CEO of The Greenleaf Center for Servant Leadership, has identified ten qualities necessary in today's servant leader.[2] If you develop these qualities, you will become the kind of leader who becomes "healthier, wiser, freer, more autonomous, and more of a servant"[3] and you will be able to lead others in this process. The ten qualities may be visualized as a triangular framework. The triangle represents three categories: contextual leadership, relational leadership, and functional leadership. Each of these categories needs to function all the time in an effective servant leader. Ignore any one or focus on any one to your peril.

> Contextual leadership focuses on interpreting reality.

Contextual leadership focuses on interpreting reality.[4] It forms the first side of the triangle. You can easily see how practical this is: a leader simply must know what is really going on before a problem can be adequately defined and strategies to tackle it are put in place. Servant leadership goes beyond symptoms to the interpretive work of discovering the real source of distress. Below are three essential qualities for contextual leadership.

Awareness: This trait involves keeping in touch with yourself, your impact on people, your organization, your community, and the people you are leading. This is an ongoing, comprehensive process. Cultivating awareness is an art and an ongoing process. Wise educators use the term "needs assessment" to encompass what this entails. We have a theory we want to teach, but to do it we have to put it into a context to which people will relate. So the preparation to teach includes the context, based on felt and actual need. It is incumbent on a leader to do the necessary, preliminary work of research, observation, and inquiry to assess the need in our organization and community. Then we go one step further

and reflect on where we stand personally in relationship to this need. Our understanding of context must be accurate, not based on our penchants, not relying solely on our experience, not based on imagination or appeal. We get down to reality; we ask the hard questions: What are my strengths and weaknesses in addressing this need? What do I need to do to equip myself to effectively meet it? How can I translate my awareness into communication my organization can clearly understand? How do I sequence this information—from simple to more complex—to ensure buy-in from all involved?

Persuasion: Servant leadership avoids even the slightest hint of coercion through pressure of personality strength or positional power. Instead we seek to influence others' thoughts, emotions, and behavior. We work toward building consensus. But to do that we simply must know the personal and organizational context of those we seek to persuade. We must learn to be a student of human behavior; what persuades one person turns off another. Think of both individuality and group dynamic when you think persuasion and you'll be on the right track. Allowing people to have a voice is one way to avoid coercion and to be an effective persuader.

Building Community: This involves assessing a community (business, ministry, or municipality) in terms of what its people need physically, socially, and functionally. This is where you apply the principles of developing the "whole person" to developing the "whole community." Building community includes identifying the virtues needed for healthy functioning and providing opportunities for people to learn to implement those virtues in a non-threatening environment. You can do this by promoting each quality of servant leadership as a virtue to be learned and practiced. For example, if your context reveals that insensitivity among co-workers is a problem, you can promote the virtue of awareness as a means to build community. You might use activities that disclose and celebrate diversity to make awareness feasible.

Relational leadership is another side of our triangular frame. Relational leadership creates and nourishes human connections among the various groups, partnerships, friendships, and networks of your community. Servant leadership works in a large part through cordial and candid conversation, which requires emotional intelligence in leaders.[5] Years ago the focus of leadership was primarily on function, "getting the job done" without consideration of the personal or emotional dimensions of the work. This strictly functional leadership style increasingly fails today. Spears' ten qualities of servant leaders reflect our human need for relationship. These qualities are:

Listening: The foundation of servant leadership, listening is closely related to awareness. It will not be easy to develop this skill because it's one that is largely "lost" in modern culture. M. Scott Peck talks in his book *The Road Less Traveled* about the ardors involved in real listening. He recalls breaking out in a sweat, developing a colossal headache, and becoming drained of all energy when he listened to a religious leader explain his beliefs. Afterward, he listened to the audience who "heard" the speaker without putting the energy into "listening." Whatever the cost in terms of time, energy, money, and change, servant leaders simply must listen to all the factions within their circles of influence. Good listeners create more good listeners! We teach through our example the behavior we want our community to habitually practice. We develop the

kind of relationships with people that motivate them to do their work with excellence and enthusiasm – a long-lasting benefit.

Empathy: This is the capacity to participate in another's feelings and ideas. Every parent probably has experienced placing a happy baby in a nursery with crying babies, and in a matter of moments, seeing their baby join the unhappy chorus. This is empathy in its simplest form. We practice it as leaders in complex adult organizations when we learn the expectations our followers have for themselves, their jobs, their bosses, and their organizations. Leaders have to learn to ask open questions to discover expectations and then build a common ground for dealing with them. The time it takes for developing empathy is more than compensated for by the avoidance of conflicts that come from unmet expectations. One result will be that our staffs will be much better equipped to deal with the unmet or unrealistic expectations of customers. Our empathy begets empathy.

Healing: In our post-modern world, leaders need to be a calming, assuring voice and an embodiment of hope. This need spans all generations and all cultures. In America, many of the young people in our workforce and churches are victims of the wreckage of families where parents lacked the time and/or the skills to

> We must learn to be a student of human behavior.

invest in the lives of their children. Hence, these young people enter the workforce and the church with deficits in motivation, purpose, and confidence. Healing begins making a positive difference in people's lives as we approach problems, conflicts, unrealized potential, and substandard work performance. A healing leader creates and maintains a sensitive and positive work environment. This makes the workplace and the church a motivating and satisfying place to be. Working in a healing leader's presence becomes a pleasure in itself.

Functional leadership is our final side of the leadership triangle. I place it last, not because it is less important, but because it is so dependent on the other two sides of the leadership triangle. To function with maximum effectiveness requires a comprehensive understanding of context and healthy relationships among leaders and people within the organization. Like many others in the servant leadership movement, I would rank its qualities as the acid test of true leadership. For this reason, I place it on the "bottom line" of our leadership triangle. The fact that the work group is productive becomes the proof that servant leadership is useful. It is not just a "feel good" leadership style. Practicing the functional leadership qualities below prevents "empty" leadership outcomes. As we work within the context of real needs and as we develop empowering relationships with our work force, these are the functional qualities we must develop. Notice their substance and depth:

> Good listeners create more good listeners!

Conceptualization: Many equate conceptualization with vision, but in reality they are not synonyms. Conceptualization is a much larger concept. It means "to see things whole, to see an end product and all that will be required to produce it." Businesses fail, ministries falter, and work languishes under a visionary leader who fails to conceptualize. To see things whole, a leader must be able to back away from day-to-day realities to focus on getting the bigger picture. Two skills crucial for strengthening one's ability to conceptualize are: 1) engaging in lifelong learning, and 2) setting the right priorities. These skills develop through reflection. We learn by ruminating on experience and ob-

taining new information. We then are able to establish priorities based on a clear understanding of our multi-faceted context.

Foresight: Whereas conceptualization results in seeing the big picture clearly, foresight is the skill that can map out how to get there. Foresight entails anticipating the consequence of certain actions and then choosing our actions to promote our purpose. We learn from both failure and success what will likely be the consequences. We learn by experience about the organization we lead. The authors of *Servant Leadership Characteristics in Organizational Life* suggest these three steps to developing foresight:

- Understand the past.
- Engage the future.
- Remove the "blinders" and develop creativity.

Stewardship: Peter Block[6] defines stewardship as "the willingness to be accountable for the well-being of the larger organization by operating in service, rather than in control, of those around us. Stated simply, it is accountability without control or compliance." Broadly speaking, stewardship involves:

- Identifying who the customers are and why we are serving them and then holding that purpose throughout our exchanges with them.
- Plotting a course of action which creates something of value for the world, our organization, and the people connected with them.
- Developing workers to become leaders in their job by giving them increased responsibility and accountability.
- Sharing power with others in the organization by ensuring they have a meaningful role to play in outcomes.

Commitment to the Growth of People:

Simply put, this means you help people win at that for which they are responsible. To be a highly functioning organization you have to recruit, build, and maintain people of the right caliber. You will attract and hold employees by being a leader who is committed to their growth. In business and in ministry, this means ensuring that people have:

• the technical skills to do every aspect of their work

• the personal skills that provide motivation for what they are doing

• the relational skills to participate in the growth of fellow workers and resolve conflict

• the business knowledge so that they can understand where their work fits into the larger picture of the organization and its purpose.

Our leadership triangle provides a structure for a broad overview of servant leadership's essential qualities. Unfortunately, these don't come to us full grown; we can't pluck them from a large "leadership tree" like ripe fruit. They are more like seeds, now planted in our souls. They are spiritually based qualities which take root as we expose ourselves to learning situations. They grow as we water them in the hard places where there are no easy answers or quick fixes. They mature as we interact with difficult people. And they are effective. They build lives, beginning with our own. They develop in us one situation and one day at a time – over a lifetime.

PERSONAL REFLECTION EXERCISE

Revisit the qualities in the three sides of the triangle for servant leadership. In each section, identify the qualities that constitute an area of strength and opportunities for growth for yourself.

Contextual Leadership:
　　Areas of strength

　　Opportunities for growth

Relational Leadership:
　　Areas of strength

　　Opportunities for growth

Functional Leadership:
　　Areas of strength

　　Opportunities for growth

2. Develop a realistic plan for how you can better use your areas of strength and create more opportunities to use them.

SMALL GROUP LEARNING TASKS

Form new small groups of three or four. Read the following Scenarios. Decide which of the three leadership skills - contextual, relational or functional — are missing. Solve the problem of what that leader must do if they are to be a servant leader in that situation. We'll gather in the large group later to hear your solutions.

Brenda has recently graduated from seminary with a degree in Christian Education. She is from a small farming community in Illinois. She has been hired by a large, urban church in Chicago that ministers primarily to street people. Brenda has designed a plan to launch a new Christian education program, but when she shares it with the people in her church they aren't interested.

John is manager of a division in a publishing company. Morale is low because the division isn't meeting productivity standards. John has a warm and open relationship with his employees. They tell him they don't have the resources to meet production standards. They think the standards aren't realistic. They feel they have not been supported by the company.

Nell is facing a performance appraisal with a problematic department head who is using company time to do personal projects. His people are carrying him by doing most of his work. Nell has critiqued this employee's work regularly, so he knows that he is not performing his job well.

NOTES

1 Robert Greenleaf, *Servant Leadership.* New York: Paulist Press, 1991, p. 13-14.

2 You can read more about them in Larry Spears' book, and the helpful pamphlet *Reflections on Leadership* and *Servant Leadership Characteristics in Organizational Life* by Don DeGraaf, Colin Tilley, and Larry Neal, available through The Greenleaf Center for servant Leadership (317) 259-1241. I relied on the qualities outlined in that pamphlet in developing this article.

3 *Servant Leadership*, p. 13-14.

4 I highly recommend Ronald Heifetz's book, *Leadership Without Easy Answers*, which gives a comprehensive understanding of adaptive (referred to in this article as "contextual") leadership.

5 Daniel Goleman, Richard Boyatzis and Annie McKee, *Primal Leadership.* Boston: Harvard Business School Press, 2002 focuses on emotional intelligence in leaders.

6 Peter Block, *Stewardship.* Berrett-Koehler: San Francisco, 1993.

The Servant Leader as Coach

by Marv Asfahl Gibbs

Summary: For the true leader, in a crisis context, priority must be placed on the needs of the person being served and serving takes precedent over leading.

What is the role of the servant leader when someone is in crisis? The process of coaching or serving as a leader when it's business as usual provides its challenges but how to serve in the crisis situation requires special consideration.

Big cities have been my home for most of my adult life. I have lived in Sao Paulo, Brazil; San Jose, Costa Rica; Santo Domingo, Dominican Republic; Miami, Florida, and now reside in the Los Angeles area. Some feel that big cities are polluted and unsafe, but I've felt my calling was best fulfilled meeting people and meeting their needs in the context of large cities.

I especially enjoy big cities such as San Francisco; it's always been one of my favorites. Carol and I were walking in the Fisherman's Wharf area on our way to dinner recently when something happened that has never occurred before, and I hope will never happen again. I felt like we were in a crowd but in fact I was caught up with the evening view of the harbor. Suddenly, a man leaped from behind a waste can and accosted us. All I could hear were his guttural sounds, and as I faced him, I saw his dirty face and dark, menacing eyes. We were alone facing a threatening situation. Adrenalin shot through my body as I prepared to confront the challenger. I was poorly equipped in terms of training or arms but we were in crisis.

> The focus isn't as much on leading as it is on serving.

Responsible for our safety, I prepared to defend my wife and myself from the attack. The truth of it was, I desperately wished someone with experience was there to guide and help us. We were in crisis. Before I tell you the rest of our story, I want to consider how a servant leader is to serve in crisis situations.

What is Servant Leadership?

Servant leadership has been defined in many ways. Greenleaf (1977), in his classic on servant leadership notes, "The servant leader is servant first" (p. 13). That

Marv Asfahl Gibbs holds two master's degrees and has lived in Latin America for 30 years, serving much of that time as Latin American Director for Young Life International. He lived with his family in Brazil, Costa Rica, and the Dominican Republic. He is currently writing his dissertation at Argosy University completing his doctorate in Organizational Leadership while living in the Los Angeles area.

concise statement vividly defines the role of the servant leader serving in a crisis situation. The priority is placed on the needs of the person being served and serving takes precedent over leading. The question faced by the servant leader is: How can personal tools and giftedness be utilized to serve the person in need? In part, the answer is found in one of the Toaist, Chuang Tzu's stories as shared by Parker Palmer in his book *The Active Life* (Palmer, 1990). Prince Wan Hui comes to his butcher and asks him how he could cut up so many oxen without dulling the blade of his ancient knife. The butcher responds,

> *The servant leader uses the tool of experience to guide and support the person in a crisis situation.*

> "There are spaces in the joints;
> The blade is thin and keen:
> When this thinness
> Finds that space
> There is all the room you need!
> It goes like a breeze!
> Hence I have this cleaver nineteen years
> As if newly sharpened!
> True, there are sometimes
> Tough joints. I feel them coming.
> I slow down, I watch closely
> Hold back, barely move the blade,
> And whump! the part falls away
> Landing like a clod of earth.
> Then I withdraw the blade,
> I stand still
> And let the joy of the work
> Sink in.
> I clean the blade
> And put it away."
> Prince Wan Hui said,
> "This is it! My cook has shown me
> How I ought to live
> My own life" (p.72-73).

As the butcher guides the blade, the servant leader seeks to guide the person in crisis as resolution is sought. The focus isn't as much on leading as it is on serving.

The Story of the Good Samaritan

Jesus tells a story of a man in a crisis situation. The story comes from Luke 10 and is known as the story of the Good Samaritan:

> *Jesus answered by telling a story.
> "There was once a man traveling from Jerusalem to Jericho. On the way he was attacked by robbers. They took his clothes, beat him up, and went off leaving him half-dead. Luckily, a priest was on his way down the same road, but when he saw him he angled across to the other side. Then a Levite religious man showed up; he also avoided the injured man. A Samaritan traveling the road came on him. When he saw the man's condition, his heart went out to him. He gave him first aid, disinfecting and bandaging his wounds. Then he lifted him onto his donkey, led him to an inn, and made him comfortable. In the morning he took out two silver coins and gave them to the innkeeper, saying, "Take good care of him. If it costs any more, put it on my bill—I'll pay you on my way back."
> "What do you think? Which of the three became a neighbor to the man attacked by robbers?" "The one who treated him kindly," the religion scholar responded. Jesus said, "Go and do the same" (Peterson, 1995, p. 172-173).*

The essential characteristics of the effective servant leader can be observed in this story. The servant leader uses the tool of experience to guide and support the person in a crisis situation as he or she seeks to understand and discover new truth and resolutions. Like the Good Samaritan, the servant leader seeks to guide as a productive resolution is sought. The resolution begins by understanding there is a crisis. The challenge is met and resolution is discovered through a guided process and the application of personal experience.

A Servant Leadership Model

Jesus concludes his parable with a question. To apply this last question to servant leadership, I would rephrase it, "What do you think? Which of the three was a servant leader? Discover the answer and go and do likewise."

Drawn from the relationship between the Samaritan and the wounded man by the side of the road, five principles of servant leadership form the basis for the "A.R.M.E.D." servant leadership paradigm. The wounded was in bad condition. He had been beaten and robbed by his fellow travelers. His societal structure had significantly damaged him. The question occurs at this point: What if he had been armed? What if someone had been present to help him when he came under attack? Perhaps the outcome would have been different. Perhaps he could have faced the crisis, and with some assistance, avoided the tragic loss of time, energy, and personal discomfort. But the story depicts him in crisis. As such, it serves as a good framework for a servant leadership paradigm, although certain considerations must first be given to the relationship and the persons involved. First, the wounded person is a person in need. This image may not be easily accepted by leaders who are accustomed to being strong and in charge. In principle, a person cannot be served unless they realize they have a need. Unless one recognizes there are ways to improve, a servant leader's effectiveness is greatly limited, or may never be utilized.

The second observation relates to the Samaritan who is in the position of a servant leader in this story. Christ casts the Samaritan in the role of a caregiver. In an effective servant leadership model, what a servant leader provides in the relationship is only given in response to recognized need. In our story, the Samaritan applied the "oil and wine." He treated the wounded man and put him on his donkey. The Samaritan provided for him through his contact with the innkeeper. And, he provided additional resources with a commitment to return and fulfill any additional obligation assumed by the injured man. The Samaritan is the source of resources and he makes those resources available to the wounded man. However, to utilize what has been offered is still the decision of the person in crisis. He could have walked out of the inn and refused the help that was made available. Since he was probably a Jew, he could have rejected the assistance offered by the Samaritan. Culturally there was a great difference between the two. But in the story, the wounded man accepted the help of the Samaritan when he recognized his need.

> *The resolution begins by understanding there is a crisis.*

The role of the servant leader is to respond to needs acknowledged by the one being served. For any person to understand his or her needs, it is necessary for one to reflect from a clear set of definitions. To look at this issue, Virgil Rowland collected responses from a large number of managers to a single question:

> *"What areas of knowledge do you feel that you yourself need to know more about to do your own management job better, to do your direction-of-people job better?"* After considerable analysis, he determined that all the answers fell into four categories as follows:
> *1. We need to know what we are supposed to do.*
> *2. We need to know how far we*

are expected to go in discharging our responsibilities and authorities.

3. We need to know how well we are expected to do our jobs.

4. We need to know how well we are doing our management jobs" (Fournies, 2000, p. 93).

It should also be noted that any parable or story has its limitations. What is intended here is to use this parable as the basis for forming a model that will serve to explain how a servant leader can be an effective tool for assisting others as they recognize their needs and seek to move forward.

The A.R.M.E.D. Paradigm

Having considered these issues and recognizing these limitations, the structure for a servant leadership paradigm is drawn from this parable. There are five parts to the A.R.M.E.D. paradigm: 1) First, the story demonstrates assessing the need as a point of beginning. 2) This is followed by resourcing. 3) The third step is moving forward or finding a way forward. 4) This is followed by empowering through networking. 5) Finally, there is the act of dedicating to support as a continuing process.

> Feedback can also serve as an effective assessment tool.

To begin, the question must be asked, how did the person get in this situation in the first place? What if the man would have been A.R.M.E.D. when he came under attack? The essence of servant leadership assumes that a person can face change and issues of alignment with greater effectiveness through the support provided by a servant leader. The implication is that the outcome could have been far different for the wounded man had he been properly prepared to meet the challenge of the robbers. He certainly would have been better off had he not been forced to face his foe alone. Through the acceptance

of servant leadership, anyone can be significantly impacted in a positive way.

Assessing

The process of servant leadership begins through initial contact with the client based on observed need. The Samaritan, in contrast to the priest and the Levite, went to the man in need and assessed what was needed. The parable says the priest and the Levite had pity on him. The unique factor in the relationship between the Samaritan and the wounded man was that the Samaritan felt more than pity, as evidenced by his actions. To make this story a perfect example of servant leadership, the Samaritan would have had a dialogue with the victim and together they would have assessed the need. In servant leadership, assessment is a discovery process based on the client's observation of his or her needs.

Thach and Heinselman present a coaching model for leadership development.

It begins with an assessment of leadership skills. This can be accomplished through a variety of means: traditional assessment center; 360° feedback; the coach conducting interviews and providing feedback; or any other method that results in quantitative and qualitative data that the leader can use to select developmental areas on which to focus. (Goldsmith, 2000. p. 226)

As an example, one of the effective tools for executive assessment is The Profile (Profile International Inc., 2000), a copyrighted assessment tool used by coaching firms. The participant is asked to answer a lengthy series of questions. Through computer-based analysis, the results are interpreted through a scale with thinking style, occupational interest, and behavioral traits being the three main categories. A profile of individual results is developed with several sub-headings under each category. This process allows values to be established on a scale from one to ten. The interpretation of these values can be an effective way to begin evaluating an executive's leadership style.

Feedback can also serve as an effective assessment tool. A rather simple form of this process is the 3X3 Coaching Model proposed by Alan Fine. He says, "The model is to give three strengths (keepers) and three weaknesses (improvements) when analyzing performance and behavior. [This approach] forces you to give balanced feedback, because you are giving three positives along with three areas to work on" (Goodsmith, 2000, p. 278).

Masterful Coaching, an executive coaching group, has suggested specific steps to the executive coaching process. As noted here, the first three steps involve assessment.

Step I. Identify leadership key roles and competencies.

Step II. Enroll your team in the process.

Step III. Conduct executive assessment interviews and 360° feedback.

Step IV. Analyze feedback and develop a plan for going forward

Step V. Create a leadership development plan with each 'A' Player and 'B' who can become an 'A.'

This is followed by executive coaching sessions which look at: 1) accomplishments, 2) what's working, 3) what's not working, and 4) what's missing that will make a difference (Masterful Coaching.com).

The implications for (Faith Based Organization) leaders are significant since assessment is commonly embraced as a platform for leadership in these organizations. In speaking of leadership in his letter to the Romans, Paul the Apostle points out the importance of assessment. "For I say, through the grace given unto me, to every man that is among you, not to think [of himself] more highly than he ought to think; but to think soberly, according as God hath dealt to every man the measure of faith" (Romans 12:3, KJV).

Resourcing

The second step in the development of a coaching relationship involves resources. In the parable, the Samaritan medicated the wounded man with oil and wine. In the ideal coaching situation, it is not the coach alone who provides resources. The coachee must also apply those resources he or she has under their control. But, for coaching to be effective, irrespective of the source, resources must be allocated to meet the needs of the person being coached. In one sense, as observed in the parable, this process requires that the coach come to the relationship with something to offer.

> Some of the most valuable resources are behavioral or attitudinal in nature.

Some of the most valuable resources are behavioral or attitudinal in nature. This approach to resourcing requires that the coach have a focus on the coachee and his or her resources, rather than on what the coach is and has to offer. This issue is addressed in *The Heart of Coaching* (Crane, 2002):

Business researchers have described a number of management approaches over the decades. Two of the most famous are Theories X and Y, articulated by Douglass McGregor… [However, today] we need a new theory. Perhaps we could call it "Theory C," for "coaching."

Theory C would hypothesize that people are motivated by:

(1) The intrinsic satisfaction of accomplishing the work itself

(2) Emotional ownership of the work, which occurs when they are allowed to be creative (and creativity can be nurtured in anyone)

(3) The opportunity to understand and contribute to goals that are meaningful to the organization

(3) Leaders and managers who provide direction (vision) rather than directions, who are honest yet compassionate in all their communications, and who challenge and support people in achieving their goals

(5) Feeling appreciated and knowing that they matter to the company they work for and to people they work with is basic to the concept of coaching.

Thus, the coachee is encouraged to discover the resources he or she has in his or her internal and surrounding environment (Crane, 2002, p. 28-29).

One of the keys to this insight is for leadership to understand what Collins (2001) identifies as the "Hedgehog Concept." In this paradigm, three circles are drawn to illustrate how passion, giftedness, and the economic engine, when integrated, come togetherto facilitate the understanding of the resources the coachee brings to the leadership situation.

> Giftedness is a resource a leader brings to any leadership situation.

More precisely, a Hedgehog Concept is a simple, crystalline concept that flows from deep understanding about the intersection of the following three circles:

1. What you can be the best in the world at (and, equally important, what you cannot be the best in the world at)? This discerning standard goes far beyond core competence. Just because you possess a core competence doesn't necessarily mean you can be the best in the world at it….

2. What drives your economic engine? All the good-to-great companies attained piercing insight into how to most effectively generate sustained and robust cash flow and profitability. In particular, they discovered the single denominator-profit per x-that had the greaest impact on their economics….

3. What you are deeply passionate about? The good-to-great companies focused on those activities that ignited their passion. The idea here is not to stimulate passion yet to discover what makes you passionate (Collins, 2001, p.95-96).

Giftedness is a resource a leader brings to any leadership situation. If the leader is gifted, it is natural that he or she will utilize those gifts in leadership. As a consequence an excellent resource is available. If the engine that drives your company is economics, and it is successful, that is a resource also available to the leadership process. Training for personnel is expensive. For that reason, in most cases an investment of financial resources is necessary to lead effectively. Collins indicates another key factor is passion. Of the three variables, this could be the most important.

Resourcing, when used in coaching, is not focused on what the coach has to offer but rather focuses on what the person who's being coached can discover in the process of meeting his or her specific needs as a leader.

In the Faith Based Organization, the application of Collins' (2000) concepts is important. Passion is a recognized necessity if leadership is to be successful at leading volunteers and staff. Again, in his letter to the Romans, Paul underlines this factor:

"Having then gifts differing according to the grace that is given to us, whether prophecy, [let us prophesy] according to the proportion of faith; Or ministry, [let us wait] on [our] ministering: or he that teacheth, on teaching; Or he that exhorteth, on exhortation: he that giveth, [let him do it] with simplicity; he that ruleth, with diligence; he that sheweth mercy, with cheerfulness" (Romans 12:6-8, KJV).

Moving Forward

The first two stages of this coaching paradigm take the coachee through an assessment process that leads to the discovery of resources that can be used in leadership. However, for change to occur, the client must be motivated and encouraged to move forward. In the case of the Good Samaritan, he put the wounded man on his donkey and they began the journey toward the inn, a place of renewal and healing.

> Among the many models for describing how human beings make progress, one uses a process of four simple stages: goals, reality, options, and the way forward…The significance of these four stages as critical variables comes from looking at how human beings and organizations make decisions. People and businesses have current situations or problems that they wish to change—their reality. They define in what way they would like this situation to be different—their goal. They then develop ways in which to close the gap between their reality and their goal—their options. Finally they commit to some action, based on the options that they have energy about and believe will create results—their way forward… (Goldsmith, 2000. p. 271-272).

In the paradigm under consideration, the question is, how can the coachee discover, through the use of the assessment process and through resourcing, a way to move toward a defined goal? It's important to note that the focus is not on arriving at this point. It is a matter of beginning to move in the right direction.

In their chapter in *Continuous Improvement in Place of Training* (Goldsmith, 2000), Liz Thach and Tom Heinselman present a model for leadership development that addresses this issue:

> *Assessment. It begins with assessment of leadership skills. The idea here is to set base, or benchmark, of current leadership competency that can be measured to determine progress.*
> *Development Plan. The next phase is the creation of a development plan or contract. Here, two things are critical. First, the leader selects only one or two high-impact areas on which to focus. Second, the leader is free to choose the goal.*
> *Public Announcement. The third phase is the public announcement. The literature describes this as "publicness" or the degree to which others are aware of the leader's goal.*
> *Implementation. Next comes the implementation step, which is comprised of developmental activities and informal follow-up with feedback participants (Goldsmith, 2000, p. 223-225).*

The phase of implementation completes the cycle, and assessment again becomes a part of the process. I prefer this model because it provides key steps and there is motion, or movement, from one stage to the next. It also provides clear steps that move the overall process forward.

> Giftedness is also vital to effective leadership in the faith-based organization.

These observations are especially apropos to the Faith-based organization (FBO) since most of the resources utilized for the work of development of the vision are generated through charitable contributions. In this case, accountability, integrity, and forward motion are key ingredients in the fulfillment of the vision. An important point in the model is the public announcement step. The FBO is a very public organization and, for that reason, commitment to objectives that are clearly defined and reported to the public are vital. Leadership in the FBO, just as in other organizations, needs to project the qualities of integrity and commitment to personal growth. The leader in an FBO lives in a very transparent world. Paul refers to the integrity issue as he looks at leadership selection in his letter to Timothy:

> *A bishop then must be blameless, the husband of one wife, vigilant, sober, of good behaviour, given to hospitality, apt to teach; Not given to wine, no striker, not greedy of filthy lucre; but patient, not a brawler, not covetous; One that ruleth well his own house, having his children in subjection with all gravity; …Moreover he must have a good report of them which are without; lest he fall into reproach… Likewise [must] the deacons [be] grave, not doubletongued, …Holding the mystery of the faith in a pure conscience (I Tim. 3:2-4, 7-9, KJV).*

In addition, Paul points out how important it is for a leader to continue to move forward with a vision to the future. "Brethren, I count not myself to have apprehended: but [this] one thing [I do], forgetting those things which are behind, and reaching forth unto those things which are before, I press toward the mark for the prize of the high calling of God in Christ Jesus" (2 Corinthians. 3:13-14, KJV).

> For change to occur, the client must be motivated and encouraged to move forward.

Empowering Through Networking

The beauty of the story of the Samaritan and the wounded man rests, in part, on the fact that the Samaritan didn't rely on his resources alone. He connected with others to help the wounded man toward his healing. The Samaritan created a network and enlisted the innkeeper to assist with the empowerment of the wounded man in his healing process.

In applying this concept to the executive world, there are three directions a coachee can be encouraged to go for help as he or she continues to move toward the desired goal. First, one may look to those in positions with supervisory responsibilities for the clarification of the vision. Second, one may look to peers as a source of alignment and feedback. And third, one may look to those the coachee is serving to discover new insights and relevant information that can actuate the decision making process:

The servant leader profile is important to consider here. Greenleaf (1977) was the father of the servant leader concept. His definition is noted here:

> *"The servant leader is servant first… It begins with the natural feeling that one wants to serve, to serve first. Then conscious choice brings one to aspire to lead. That person is sharply different from one who is leader first, perhaps because of the need to assuage an unusual power drive or to acquire material possessions. For such it will be a late choice to serve after leadership is established. The leader-first and the servant first are two extreme types… The best test, and difficult to administer, is: Do those served grow as persons? Do they, while being served, become healthier, wiser, freer, more autonomous, more likely themselves to become servants?" (Greenleaf, 1977, p. 13-14).*

Coaching toward servant leadership is best modeled by the coach in his or her relationship with the leader being coached. The discovery of the servant leader reality may not be found within oneself at first. However, if the coach models this style of leadership, it can be discovered. In leadership, the systemic model is often based on the human body. Each part is seen as having a function and should be empowered to function as part of the body or team:

> *For as the body is one, and hath many members, and all the members of that one body, being many, are one body...whether [we be] Jews or Gentiles, whether [we be] bond or free; ...For the body is not one member, but many. If the foot shall say, Because I am not the hand, I am not of the body; is it therefore not of the body? And if the ear shall say, Because I am not the eye, I am not of the body; is it therefore not of the body? If the whole body [were] an eye, where [were] the hearing? If the whole [were] hearing, where [were] the smelling? (I Corinthians 12: 12-17, KJV).*

In the faith-based organization, in addition to an emphasis on working as a body, the training element of networking is a vital part of the leadership structure. Members are encouraged to learn from, and teach each other, as giftedness is expressed within the organization. In Paul's writing, he addressed this issue of leadership with Timothy, his protégé. He is encouraged to be about the task of networking. "...The things that thou hast heard of me among many witnesses, the same commit thou to faithful men, who shall be able to teach others also" (II Timothy 2:1-2, KJV).

Dedicated to Support

The final stage of the paradigm is con-

tinuing support. Here the focus is on the action of the coach. The Samaritan made arrangements with the innkeeper and committed to return. This implied his continued support to the process that would carry the wounded man toward his goal of complete health. As noted by Goldsmith, effective support for leadership development should be based in a...Continuous Learning Philosophy... It is important to think about "following" the process versus "completing" the process. As in Deming's PDCA (Plan-Do-Check-Act) process (Deming, 1982) of continuous quality improvement, one never completes it. It is a way of life; it's how one goes about work...leadership development is not to be viewed as another task to be accomplished but rather a different way to go about work. Learning must be seen as a life process, not a task" (Goldsmith, 2000, p. 228).

While these comments may be aimed at the coachee and the relationship to his or her organization, they also imply that a relationship with a coach is not focused on a completed task but is seen as a life process that will probably involve a long-term relationship.

In every organization servant leaders are responsible to be dedicated to the support of those who are under their supervision. This principle applies when a group is given authority to move forward as a team or when a person is casting vision.

> The discovery of the servant leader reality may not be found within oneself at first.

This concept is illustrated in Paul's writings to Titus. Titus was one of the leaders Paul left in charge of a developing community as he moved through Asia Minor establishing small groups or churches. He writes: "For this cause left I thee in Crete, that thou shouldest set in order the things that are wanting, and ordain elders in every city, as I had appointed thee:

If any be blameless, the husband of one wife, having faithful children not accused of riot or unruly" (Titus 1: 5-6, KJV).

Paul also left us a model of dedication to continuing support as he writes to the church at Corinth. In this writing, he mentions the number of times he has visited before and suggests that he will visit again in the future. He is holding the leadership accountable and suggests an orderly manner to deal with differences. "This [is] the third [time] I am coming to you. In the mouth of two or three witnesses shall every word be established. I told you before, and foretell you, as if I were present, the second time; and being absent now I write …that, if I come again, I will not spare..." (II Cor. 13:1-3, KJV).

Conclusion

The A.R.M.E.D. model for servant leadership is designed to illustrate the steps to be utilized in effective coaching. It is important to note that while the concluding point in the model is focused on continuing support, the goal through the coaching process is to bring leaders to a new level of self-discovery and competence. David Allen presents what he calls an "old behavioral model" for measuring competency in his chapter in *Coaching for Leadership* (Goldsmith, 2002):

1. Unconscious Incompetence: "I don't even know that I don't know what I don't know."

> The faith-based organization is like any other organization and is in need of coaching.

2. Conscious Incompetence: "I now know where I ought to be and what I ought to be doing, but I don't know how to get myself there or how to get myself to do it."

3. Conscious Competence: "I know now how to make it happen and I know I can do it, but I have to keep reminding myself to stay on track."

4. Unconscious Competence: "I just do it. I only think about it when I don't do it, and then I have to go do it" (Goodsmith, 2000, p. 233).

Dr. Andrea Molberg (2003) suggests there is a fifth level is a great asset for servant leaders who seek to achieve in ourselves and those we are coaching. That level is a Conscious Unconscious Competence. This level allows us to look at our competence and rationally share with others those things we practice at our unconscious competence level.

In the practice of metacognition we are able to think about the way we think. At the Conscious Unconscious Competence level, we are able to think about the way we coach as we lead from the Unconscious Competence level.

This fifth level is a great asset and leads those who seek excellence in coaching. The goal is for those being coached to reach a level where they are independent to serve others. That may never be fully achieved in a successful FBO.

Bob was one of my coaches for about 15 years while I worked in Latin America with Young Life International. He lives in Colorado but stopped by the other day on his way to a conference near Los Angeles. We hadn't seen each other for some time and are no longer in the same organization. The depth to which our relationship has gone was illustrated by the warmth of our conversation. We shared about our dreams and visions until almost midnight. He was an excellent coach. He still is, and I always enjoy it when he helps me think about my life and my work, even now as I consider launching a new faith-based organization.

"The Rest of the Story"

Oh, by the way, remember the experience I shared at the beginning of the article when my wife and I were "attacked" by this strange man on Fisherman's Wharf in

San Francisco? The whole experience was a "set-up!" A street-person hid behind a waste can with some greenery as his camouflage. When an unsuspecting person walked by he would jump out and scare them. Everyone standing around knew what was happening because they too had been through the experience. As we jumped to get out of the man's grasp, everyone laughed: "He'd managed to scare another couple, and that was a good one!" We were so shaken we didn't stay around to see what happened to other unsuspecting victims. It was all in fun, but certainly provided me with an experience for reflection! If someone with a servant heart who'd been through the experience could have coached me the experience certainly would have been different.

PERSONAL REFLECTION EXERCISE

Identify some of the people who have served as a coach to you in the past. Describe these people and the impact their coaching had on you.

From your own experience, what motivates you to be an empowering coach?

SMALL GROUP LEARNING TASKS

Form new small groups of four. Read Karl Wood's story. Answer the questions that follow. Later you will have the opportunity to share your answers in the large group.

Karl Wood's Story

Karl has just relocated his young family to Thailand to lead a team of people who are going to do community building in the rural sections of the north. Karl is impassioned about this work and has had ten years of community building in another area in Thailand. However, when he begins to work with the team, he is frustrated to discover that most of them lack community building experience. Some lack the confidence to delegate. They are unrealistic about what they can accomplish the first year and are weighed down by the burden of not having "enough hours in the day."

1. What is Karl dealing with?

2. Why do you think it happens?

3. When something like this happens in your situation, what problems will it cause?

4. What coaching opportunities does this situation present to Karl?

The Dance of Servant Leadership

by Judy Gomoll

Summary: In Jesus' upside down approach to leadership, he demonstrates a servanthood that is distinct in its motivation: a simple desire to serve because of an unconditional love.

"The servant leader is servant first.... It begins with the natural feelings that one wants to serve, to serve first. Then conscious choice brings one to aspire to lead. That person is sharply different from one who is leader first.... The difference manifests itself in the care taken by the servant first to make sure that other people's highest priority needs are being served."—Robert K. Greenleaf, *Servant Leadership*, p. 13.

Jesus told them, "In this world the kings and great men order their people around, and yet they are called 'friends of the people.' But among you, those who are the greatest should take the lowest rank, and the leaders should be like a servant. Normally the master sits at the table and is served by his servants. But not here! For I am your servant."—Luke 22:25-27, New Living Translation

My husband and I were living in Africa in 1999 when I began a graduate program in Leadership Studies. One day a Kenyan friend asked me, "Why study leadership? Do you hold a leadership position in your mission agency?"

I replied, "I guess because this topic interests me, especially in light of the corruption and genocide devastating so many African societies today at the hands of contemptible leaders. But, no, I don't hold a leadership position. In fact, I usually do not conceive of myself as a leader."

My friend was shocked by my reply. "Of course you are a leader," he insisted, "and I can name at least a dozen emerging leaders who regard you as their mentor. If you're not a leader, then what are you?"

At issue back then was neither my organizational position nor my contribution to God's work. It was my concept of leadership that was wanting. As an introvert and a missionary wife living in an obscure town in central Kenya, I simply did not fit my own caricature of leaders: up

> As an introvert and a missionary wife living in an obscure town in central Kenya, I simply did not fit my own caricature of leaders.

Judy Gomoll serves on the National Staff Training Team for The Navigators as a mentor, coach, and writer. Currently she is passionate about writing a new spiritual formation Bible study series for a post modern, pluralistic audience. She holds a master's degree in organizational leadership from Azusa Pacific University. She and her husband made their home in Uganda and Kenya for fifteen years.

front, charismatic, visionary, direction-setting, intuitively and unquestioningly knowing the right thing to do, always focusing on the forest rather than the trees. For years I had rather awkwardly avoided the "dance" of leadership. So my friend's loving rebuke launched me on a quest to answer the question: If not a leader, then what was I?

> **What is it about a servant leader that attracts followers?**

In the intervening years, my understanding of leadership—especially servant leadership—has developed a great deal. In this article I will clarify what I believe servant leadership is by exploring six questions:

What is at the heart of servant leadership?

A servant leader both serves and leads. How can she combine both functions without diminishing either?

Is a Christian called to be a leader who serves, or to be a servant who leads? What differences does this distinction make?

What impact will genuine servant leadership have on the servant leader herself?

What impact will genuine servant leadership have on others?

What is it about a servant leader that attracts followers?

What is at the heart of servant leadership?

> *"Capacity and competence are like gliders. They can fly, but not indefinitely. And they might not hold up during turbulent times. Who you are will take you much further than what you can do (capacity and competence). Character will stand the test of time and hold up when the wind howls and the storm rages around you." – (David Kraft, pp. 75-76, paraphrasing Gordon MacDonald, p. 57)*

At the heart of servant leadership is character—not capacity or competence or know-how or know-who. As important as competency is in all fields, it is ultimately overshadowed by one's character in the eyes of followers when the tough decision have to be made. One need look no further than the daily newspaper to discover how quickly we reject leaders—even highly competent leaders—who lack integrity and character. Research (Posner and Schmidt, 1984, 1986) confirms that the primary quality followers look for and admire in their leaders is integrity, a quality encompassing truthfulness, trustworthiness, character and convictions. This research revealed competence as a second most admired quality. Perhaps one lesson to be learned from the research is that trustworthiness unleashes a leader's influence among followers. Or to be more blunt, a leader will not make it without trust, and trust will not happen without sound character.

This is what distinguishes servant leadership from the other leadership "flavors-of-the-month." The servant leader views her leadership as influence flowing from who she is in her essential character rather than as power flowing from her role or what she can do. We all know of people who have exerted tremendous influence for good without having any particular title or official role, people who recognized the needs of others and moved authentically and often sacrificially and without fanfare to meet those needs. They are the humble heroes in the servant leadership hall of fame.

How can a leader combine both serving and leading without diminishing either?

During a leadership workshop I attended, participants were asked to draw a picture of the leadership style they were most familiar with. Some drew a pyramid representing a hierarchical leadership style. Others drew a staff depicting shepherd leadership. Others drew fish in a large net to portray participatory leadership. A few sought an image to capture the essence of servant leadership. I argued that servant leadership is not just another entrée option on the leadership menu. For a follower of Jesus Christ—the consummate servant leader—it is the only option. But what does it really look like?

Perhaps another way to address this question is to ask: When Jesus knelt down with a basin and washed the dusty feet of his disciples just before his death, was he primarily leading or primarily serving? What motivated him? I suggest that he was both serving and leading simultaneously and equally. As their leader, he was setting an example for them to follow. But his act of service was not motivated primarily by a desire to model (i.e., to lead by example). He was motivated by a desire to serve people simply because he loved them. The motive makes all the difference.

What is wrong with doing something out of a desire to model exemplary behavior for others? Answer: Potentially the same thing that was wrong with the Pharisees' verbose public praying on street corners. They may have been "modeling" prayer for their followers, but one wonders who they were actually talking to. It is the same thing that is wrong with my own tendency to do personal evangelism only when someone I am discipling is in tow. Watch out when one's primary motivation to serve springs from a "leaderly" desire to set a good example more than from a servant's sincere heart to meet the needs of others in love.

The principle here is that a servant leader must beware of serving as "show." Servant leadership cannot be forced or feign the appearance of humility. Rather genuine servant leadership flows from the primary value of serving other people's priority needs. It is motivated first by love—not by the desire to model. This helps to keep serving and leading in balance.

Perhaps this illustration will clarify what difference motive makes. A highly-placed business

> A leader will not make it without trust, and trust will not happen without sound character.

executive, who readily identified himself as a leader who serves, was boasting to a friend of mine[1] about his company's commitment to servant leadership.

Friend: Why is your for-profit organization committed to something like servant leadership?

Executive: It leads to a flatter organization and more inclusive decision-making.

Friend: Why do you want that?

Executive: Well, our employees like it. And it empowers people.

Friend: Why do you want that?

Executive: (starting to get flustered) Well. . .there's less pressure and it helps our retention rate.

Friend: And why do you want that?

Executive: You're really pushing me here...and I think I know where you're going.

Friend: Where do you think we are going?

Executive: (after a long pause) Actually, we want all that because our employees work harder, and our profits increase, and we look good in the eyes of the investors, and I get a bigger bonus.

Friend: Now that's honest of you. Let me ask one more question. If your company began to struggle with the bottom line in terms of profits and losses, and you felt that servant leadership was part of the reason, would you jettison it?

Executive: It would be gone in a week.

So much of what we call servant leadership is just a kinder form of leading that hopefully coerces people to work harder and produce more. And it can be found in religious settings as readily as in corporate contexts. It is self-serving at its core, unlike Jesus whose motive was not "to be served, but to serve" even when the bottom line was death.

Is a Christian called to be a leader who serves, or to be a servant who leads? What difference does this distinction make?

> What is wrong with doing something out of a desire to model exemplary behavior for others?

In addition to the motive of love, I believe that it is critical for a leader to distinguish between identity and function... between who I am and what I do. The issue here is not motive, but identity. I would make the case that a Christian should view herself as a servant of God who leads rather than as a leader of people who serves. The first reason is because Jesus so viewed himself. For hundreds of years, Jewish prophets had foretold the Servant of the Lord who would come to save God's people. Jesus' identity was as a servant first of all (Luke 22:27, Philippians 2:7). He was a servant so secure in his identity, so unconcerned about his status or how he looked to people that he was totally free to move authentically and humbly beyond the boundaries that usually define—and confine—a leader's behavior. I believe that the freedom flowing from one's self-concept as a servant first is rarely available to the person who thinks of herself primarily as a leader first—even a leader who serves.

The story is familiar. On the night he was betrayed, Jesus served his disciples by washing their feet—normally the act of a menial servant. The Message translation of the Bible tells the story this way:

"So he got up from the supper table, set aside his robe, and put on an apron. Then he poured water into a basin and began to wash the feet of the disciples, drying them with his apron. When he got to Simon Peter, Peter said, "Master, you wash my feet?" (John 13:4-6)

This un-leaderly-like behavior on the part of Jesus was too out-of-the-box for Peter. Had Jesus been operating out of a leader-first identity, he might have chosen to summon the owner of the home and request that a household servant be sent to take care of this customary guest service. In that case, Peter would probably not have been so undone; he might have missed Jesus' point.

The text reveals where Jesus found the freedom to be a servant first. Verse 3 describes his sense of identity this way:

"Jesus knew that the Father had put him in complete charge of everything, that he came from God and was on his way back to God" (John 13:3, MSG).

Jesus had an unshakable confidence in his own identity. He knew who he was, and whose servant he was. God was his only master; what he did for his beloved disciples, he did in service to his Father. In so doing, he "elevated [this] humble physical gesture to express his own servant heart, which would lead him to the cross" in just a matter of hours[2] —the ultimate act of servant leadership.

When I see my identity as a leader first and my task being that of service, I will probably limit myself to doing only leader-like acts of service—things like pharisaical praying and modeling-motivated evangelism. Something tells me that each has already received any due reward. The only way to blend leading with serving without sacrificing either on the altar of expediency is to keep my identity clearly distinguishable from my task. I am a servant who leads, and in this identity there is great freedom.

What impact will genuine servant leadership have on the servant leader herself?

That leads us to the third question: How will one's core identity as a servant first and one's core motive of love impact the servant leader? Ironically, I see the most significant impact as being amazing freedom. Why ironic? Because the one mark of a servant (many of whom were actually slaves in earlier eras) is that she is at the beck and call of her master, with very little freedom over her time or her tasks.

Few westerners have actually had personal experience with domestic servants. During our years in Africa we employed a series of "house helpers," without whom our daily routines would have been immeasurably more difficult. Grace Mutonyi was a shy 17-year-old grade-school dropout from a small village in eastern Uganda when she came to work in our home. For the next twelve years—during which she married and gave birth to two children—Grace did whatever I asked her to do whenever I asked her to do it. Until the day we left Uganda, she cooked, cleaned, shopped, and prayed for us and for the scores of better educated and more upwardly mobile Ugandan university students who shared our home and our hearts. Her quiet service belied her tremendous influence. No one has "taught" me more about Christlike servanthood than Grace. Today, as the wife of a humble pastor, Grace disciples more women and counsels more couples and leads more people to the Lord (including several Muslim women and their families) than most missionaries I know, including myself. She illustrates the principle that, when someone with a servant identity leads people, tremendous power is unleashed.

What impact will genuine servant leadership have on others?

Those who rub shoulders with a genuine servant leader cannot help but be affected. The servant leader's freedom releases the aroma of Christ and the power of God to those around them. Here's a true story that illustrates this point:

There was a man who, for financial reasons, had to quit medical school one year short of receiving his degree. But his outstanding skills earned him a prestigious position as a tutor at the Harvard Medical School. One day he was supervising medical students who were dissecting their first cadavers. One squeamish student accidentally spilled a heap of internal organs and sloppy tissue onto the floor of the lab. Since the janitor was nowhere in sight, and because he did not want his students distracted from the learning task at hand, the tutor instinctively grabbed a bucket, got down on his knees, and cleaned up the mess. Then he got back to his tutoring as if nothing extraordinary had happened.

His simple act of service jarred the perceptions of many. One distinguished older professor pulled him aside and reprimanded him sternly. "Don't ever do that again! Do you see the name tags you and I both wear? They read: 'Harvard Medical School Faculty.' I gave my life to get this name tag, and you will not degrade it. Faculty members don't wipe floors or carry buckets. People will lose respect for us."

As you can imagine, the tutor became the talk of the school community. The next night when the tutor met for Bible study with some of the students, ten new students came for

> Genuine servant leadership flows from the primary value of serving other people's priority needs.

the first time, no doubt drawn by curiosity and the aroma of Christ emanating from this servant leader. Five days later, the same professor drew the tutor aside again, and said, "I've been looking for you. Your act of cleaning up that mess has caused me sleepless nights. I can't figure you out. I could never do what you did. How can you be so free—and yet also be so capable in your field and so appreciated by the students? What gives you such freedom? Wherever you get it, I want that freedom, too." Before long, the professor was reading the Bible under the "tutelage" of the tutor.

Two hindrances to servant leadership are the desire to be seen and recognized as a leader and the false belief that acts of humble service will diminish us in the eyes of others. Biblical servant leadership, however, produces freedom in the leader and holiness in others when the person who should be elevated chooses instead to serve in love. When we bring our core identity as a servant with only one master into whatever we do—leading, teaching, coaching, driving a truck, screening luggage—we are freed to do almost anything and God blesses those around us by releasing the aroma of Christ far beyond our roles or lack thereof and deep into our spheres of influence.

> So much of what we call servant leadership is just a kinder form of leading that hopefully coerces people to work harder and produce more.

What is it about a servant leader that attracts followers?

The question of why people follow leaders is an important one. In Africa, corrupt leaders from every conceivable walk of life and faith community attract followers through an implicit and explicit system of bribery, paternalism, and intimidation— vices shared by westerners, of course. Many people follow leaders out of intimidation or because they have something to gain from the association. If leaders could choose, most would prefer that people follow them because they want to rather than following because they have to. So the question remains: what is it about servant leadership that prompts people to want to follow the servant leader?

Again, Jesus' servant leader approach provides one important answer. When he went about leading the world back to the Father, he chose absolutely upside down methods—methods that would certainly not get him elected to any political post in our country. To put it mildly, he had almost nothing "leaderly" going for him. Consider these untarnished facts about his background and life:

Birthplace—an unsanitary barn in an obscure town

Parentage—worse than obscure, many regarded him as an illegitimate child

Ancestry—an extended family past checkered with the likes of gentiles, prostitutes, cheats, womanizers, and worse

Arrival—a let-down witnessed by a motley crew of nobodies

Name—common enough to be easily forgettable

Appearance—as ordinary and forgettable as his name

Hometown—of dubious reputation

Socio-economic status—poor, sometimes homeless, oblivious to the need for financial planning

Advance man—undignified, abrasive, inappropriately dressed, and committed to organic foods

Cabinet members—mostly blue collar laborers with no special skills for this line of work

Followers—drawn from the ranks of the sordid, desperate, violent, crafty, marginalized, and sensual

Death—outrageously shameful and degrading execution[3]

Jesus was distinctly "uncredentialed" to be a leader, at least from the world's perspective. But he was just what one might expect for a servant—or a slave. The genius of Jesus' upside down approach to leadership was that there was not an iota of intimidation about him, nothing in his background or lifestyle to threaten or manipulate followers with, nothing to coerce or bribe even the worst off member of the human race to follow him for any of the wrong reasons. Nobody—absolutely nobody—feels obligated to follow a leader like that. Jesus' servant personhood was so unintimidating that the only reason people followed him was because they trusted him. There was simply nothing in it for them—other than a relationship. And that is the point. Today only those genuinely hungering for a relationship with the Divine bother to apply.

Herein lies the secret power of genuine, humble, biblical servant leadership—his and ours. How seemingly un-godlike! How non-threatening! How oblivious to political correctness! There is nothing about Jesus designed to impress us or in danger of scaring us off, no material rewards making us put on masks in hopes of being chosen for his team. Jesus sees the forest of humanity, but he cherishes every "tree" among us.

By coming to us as a humble servant, Jesus is approachable, available—even vulnerable—to the likes of us. Better yet, he is reaching out to touch us, wounds and all. Unlike other men, he does not retreat uncomfortably from our scars and tears and neediness. Instead, unlike most leaders, he lets us touch his scars and taste his tears. What an upside down God Jesus is!

So I was wooed by the servant of all to join the "dance" of leadership. He may not be the best-looking guy or the slickest dancer on the floor, either of which would have sent this wallflower escaping to the girls' room to avoid the humiliation of not being chosen. Instead, this genuine, authentic Jesus steps up almost unnoticed beside me, smiles, and says invitingly, "Shall we dance? I'll lead, and you can follow." In his crazy, wonderful upside down Kingdom I am free to choose him—and free to follow in his footsteps as a servant who leads.

NOTES

1 Paul Stanley, Vice President of The Navigators, told me this story.

2 Ryken, L., J. Wilhoit, and T. Longman, eds. *Dictionary of Biblical Imagery*, Downers Grove, IL: Inter Varsity Press, 1998, p. 926.

3 Adapted from Erwin, pp. 7-24.

PERSONAL REFLECTION EXERCISE

1. Describe an instance where you served with self-serving motives. What impact did this have upon you and other/s served?

2. Now describe an instance of the opposite, where you served with the motive to enhance the life of others. What impact did this have upon you and the other/s served?

3. Compare the two outcomes. What do you discover?

SMALL GROUP LEARNING TASK

Form new small groups of no more than four.

On the following page are listed customary uses of the word "Service" identified by the Robert K. Greenleaf Center. For each of these uses, answer the questions:

What would self-serving service look like in that situation?

What would other-serving service look like in that situation?

Customer Service. The customer's satisfaction is most important in the provision of goods.

Personal Service. For a fee or charge, something of value is offered upon request (e.g. accounting medical, legal, counseling, hairdresser, etc.).

Public Service. Tax supported general amenities (e.g. roads, sewer systems, water, parks, fire protection, police protection, electric power, libraries, etc.).

Human Service. Public-supported responses to people's crisis or long-term dependency needs.

Voluntary Service. Non-governmental sponsored responses to individual and family crisis or circumstances.

Relief Services. Direct aid following disasters, emergencies and the direct assistance for individuals living in chronic poverty.

Military Service. Defending the country.

Worship Service. Religious organizations acknowledging that which hold up as most worthwhile.

Developmental Service. Focus on growth, self esteem and capacity building of persons seeking assistance towards becoming more self-reliant and able to contribute to th4e social group.

Indentured Service. Slavery or the holding of someone to do your bidding of terms.

Community Service. A judge's requirement for convicted persons as a required sentence.

Environmental Service. The universe serves us as we serve the earth.

REFERENCES

Erwin, G. D., (1988). *The Jesus Style.* Dallas, TX: Word Publishing.

Greenleaf, Robert K. (1977). *Servant leadership: A journey into the nature of legitimate power and greatness.* New York: Paulist Press.

Holy Bible: New Living Translation. (1996). Wheaton, IL: Tyndale House Publishers, Inc.

Kraft, D. (2004). *Leaders who last: Learning to live and lead differently.* Edmonds, WA: Timeline Books.

MacDonald, G. (2003, Winter). *The root of leadership: How to gain and maintain your people's trust.* Leadership, 24(1), 55-64.

Peterson, Eugene H. (2002). *The Message: The Bible in contemporary language.* Colorado Springs, CO: NavPress.

Posner, B. Z., & Schmidt, W. H. (1986). *Values and expectations of federal service executives.* Public Administration Review, 46(5), 447-454.

Posner, B. Z., & Schmidt, W. H. (1984). *Values and the American manager: An update.* California Management Review, 26(3), 202-216.

Ryken, L., Wilhoit, J. & Longman, T. (Eds.). (1998), *Dictionary of biblical imagery.* Downers Grove, IL: InterVarsity Press.

Stanley, Paul. Personal interview. August 23, 2005. Colorado Springs, CO.

Standing Upright in the Wind:

Servant Leader Choices

by Keith D. Walker

Summary: Servant leaders can find their balance when they employ ethical discernment, ethical determination, ethical deliberation, and ethical diligence.

Introduction

Making ethical decisions is important to each one of us who value servant leadership. It is especially important for leaders in their formative first five years in a new profession. For the neophyte leader, moral habits and ethical decision patterns are formed for an entire professional tenure during these years. This is not to say we become hard-wired, but we do habituate ethical interactions, responses, and choices in subtle, incremental patterns. At a minimum, aspiring to be or "professing" to be a servant leader builds on the platform of integrity and is mediated by one's character and competence. It is just as important to those "long-in-the-tooth" who will know the importance of ethical keen-ness and the critical—no, the essential—requirement of constant ethical renewal and vigilance. For those who have sought to exercise servant leadership for many years the challenge is to examine their practice, reaffirm their principles, and influence those around them to think, do, and act with ethical integrity. Based on the findings from a reliable research project (Josephson Institute for Advancement of Ethics), certain things are predictable:

> *Most people believe that their personal ethical standards are higher than those generally found in society.*

> *That every reader of this article would say that they want, in their heart of hearts, to be an ethical person*

> *That each of us also wants to be thought of as highly ethical*

> *That most of us would say, if asked, that we believe others are not quite as ethical as they should be*

> *That most people believe that their personal ethical standards are higher than those generally found in society*

> *That most believe that their occupation, whether as a servant leader with business, social or public sector responsibilities is more ethical than*

Keith Walker, Ph.D., is Professor of Educational Administration and Leadership at the University of Saskatchewan in Canada. Keith is an avid leadership researcher and loves to facilitate learning and dialogue about leadership and followership. His current interests revolve around notions of fostering trust and hope, as well as leading in the new economy, personal and spiritual lives of leaders, and building our capacity for authentic and appreciative learning communities.

other professions/occupations.

The research would also suggest that in an organization of good people (such as the one you work in), most would believe themselves to be personally and professionally more ethical than the other members of the organization, working under the same auspices, and with similar super-ordinate purposes.

I want to introduce this topic by affirming us—author and reader—as well intentioned and typically upright people. At the same time, I'd like to affirm our desire to sustain our uprightness when the situational winds of pressure confront and threaten to tip us. Likewise, the organizations that you work with make many efforts to sustain their earned and deserved reputations of integrity and ethics. It is an appropriate beginning to think the best of each other. In the main, these positive self-images help to sustain our ethical "tonus." On the other hand, I would invite you to join me in my admission that while I aspire to be good, right, virtuous, and proper, I sometimes struggle with what may be called an "internal civil war." I know what is right, good, virtuous, and proper but sometimes fail to live up to my own standards. I am sometimes surprised that there is an inner battle for things that ought to be pre-decided, but there is.

> Throughout our lives, we learn from experience and build pictures of what it means to be ethical.

I would like to suggest that there are good reasons not to leave the matters of ethics leadership with no more said than this. I would like to explore the area under four headings:

Ethical Discernment
Ethical Determination
Ethical Deliberation
Ethical Diligence

Each of these could easily constitute the topic for a complete article, or for a one day workshop, but my purpose here is to do no more than raise and consider some basic ideas.

Let's put some personal relevance and substance into these ideas before discussing them more fully. Pause for a moment from your reading and bring to your mind someone for whom you have a tremendous amount of ethical respect. We all know somebody fitting that description. These people often personify your tangible images of servant leadership. If we think about them, we can probably "see" or "hear" them quite clearly, even if they are not with us.

Ask yourself, "What is it about that person that singled them out for you, that brought them to mind? What are the features of their ethicality? What characterizes their servant likeness?" We all seem to have an in-built ability to know what it takes to be an ethical person. I don't think this is just a subjective thing. Throughout our lives, we learn from experience and build pictures of what it means to be ethical. That picture helps us with our discernment and our ability to help those in our organization who look to us for ethical leadership.

Servant leadership involves reflecting on ethicality in a very conscious way. Ethics pervades everything we do. As servant leaders we are in the people business, and ethics is embedded in that. Are there any people decisions that we make as leaders which do not have some possible positive or negative ethical ramifications? If you can think of one, let me know.

However, in the field where I work with undergraduate and postgraduate students in educational administration and leadership, the emphasis tends to be on subjects such as the politics of education, organizational theory, human resources management, financial management, organizational development, and public relations. These are undeniably important to the work that we do, but what of ethics? Far from being dealt with in a way that reflects our need to be explicitly and discernibly ethical in our professional orientation and practice, ethics tends to have been implicit and assumed in our pre-service and in-service courses. We need to become more explicit about ethicality in our training, practice, and personal behaviour, if we are to provide suitable ethical models and lead by example.

Ethical Discernment

What we don't know about each other is how satisfied we are with our present state of ethical fitness (personally, professionally, and organizationally). We also don't know exactly what will be required of us tomorrow. These internal and external variables warrant our thinking about ethics in a discreet fashion.

Through experience and wisdom, there are some who have come to a state of what might be called "authentic ethical humility"—knowing that there is always room to grow in the ethical realm and wanting to be better today than yesterday, and better still tomorrow. When at their best, these people realize that they don't have to be ethically sick or corrupt to get ethically better.

Experience teaches us a great deal. We often get our ethical consciousness or moral sensitivity through events or circumstances along life's way. Displacement of "ethical muteness," moral complacency or even ethical mediocrity, is best achieved in a proactive fashion rather than in response to difficult circumstances. Be assured, if you are new in the exercise of leadership, difficult situations and challenging issues will visit you! It only takes one or two of these to appreciate one's own frailties, fragilities, and the precarious days in which we live.

I am reminded of Darley and Batson's work in moral psychology. These two researchers worked in the mid-1970s with seminarians preparing for the ministry at Princeton Theological Seminary. The seminarians were asked to prepare and deliver a short talk on the parable of the Good Samaritan, and then to deliver their talks in another building, requiring a short walk between campus buildings. Darley and Batson used the walk as an analogy of the famous road between Jerusalem and Jericho, and to complete the scenario, positioned a student confederate along the way, who was slumped over, shabbily dressed, coughing and groaning. Darley and Batson wanted to see how each of the subjects would respond to the "victim."

The factor that made a large difference in helping behaviour was the time pressure put on the subjects. Those seminarians who were placed under great pressure tended to help less than the seminarians who were given a more leisurely pace to compose and deliver their short talks.

The seminarians under pressure seemed not to have processed the new situation (the "victim") since they were so absorbed with fulfilling

> As servant leaders we are in the people business, and ethics is embedded in that.

their first duty—preparing the talk and getting to the other building for their presentation on time. Indeed, several seminary students literally stepped over the victim as they hurried off to speak on the parable of the Good Samaritan.

When I think about this study, it reminds me that I too can fail to meet ethical obligations on my way to do a good deed. I intend to serve but haven't left sufficient margins in my life to do so. I don't think there is room to be sanguine when it comes to ethics in leadership. Busy lifestyles, pressured lives, and even enthusiasm to do good can distract us from discerning the first order needs of those around us and our call to direct ethical behaviour.

Ethical Discernment and Servant Leadership

As aspiring servant leaders, we are a good, well-intentioned bunch of people, aren't we? Is that not how we see ourselves? And are not the people who work for and with us similarly well-intentioned? We are a good cadre, on our way to doing good, but there are so many things along the way that we need to beware of, to be discerning about.

Step outside your reading again for a moment and personalize this: Imagine several of the people you know from your workplace who might be reading this article (see boldfaced text above). Ask yourself how many of these people would have thought of you as an ethical person, servant leader, for whom they have great respect. If they know you, they will have been able to make an assessment on the basis of decisions they have seen you make, together with their images of the ethical attitudes you have made explicit.

When I ask myself this question, suddenly I understand the meaning of "ethical humility." I would like to be thought of in this way, but I am not confident that I have yet reached this point in the eyes of the colleagues who know me best. A key characteristic of servanthood is humility. Without humility there is no grace; without grace there is no authenticity or consistency in one's service to others.

Frequently others are involved with our decision-making even if we do not consciously include them. We do not, and should not, operate in isolation. We need to

> *Busy lifestyles, pressured lives, and even enthusiasm to do good can distract us from discerning the first order needs of those around us.*

pace ourselves, and recognize that there are many times when we cannot do it all on our own. We all require the help of others. Other people have different sets of "antennae" beyond those that we have built into our personal ethical "handbook."

Collaborative ethical decision-making is so important. A "lone servant leader" is a contradiction in terms. How often there needs to be somebody on hand to ask questions like "Is anybody going to be hurt by this decision?" or, perhaps more pragmatically, "How will this look if it is covered in the newspapers?" We need more than just ourselves involved in the discernment process.

Ethical Discernment in a Broader Context

Where a state is based on the consent of the governed, every citizen or stakeholder is entitled to have complete confidence in the integrity of those who purport to serve them. Each agent of the state, parents, police, employing board, and the general public, must help to earn that trust, and must honour it, by his or her integrity and conduct in all private and official action.

The challenges associated with working as a servant leader requires a great sense of discernment. Not only do we need knowledge of laws, rules, and standards applicable to our organizational-community settings, but we need to be able to access the best and most reliable information and data upon which to base our decision. We are living in the so-called "Knowledge Age." Not everything out there is true, reliable, good, and beautiful. We need to be discerning.

We need to link up with people who are especially adept at detecting trends and issues that enable us to be proactive—people who can help us understand and interpret our world. We need to build discerning, professional, learning communities, with people of conscience and critique, commitment and covenant.

Leaders make space for the discerning. They foster organizational cultures that make room for ethical sensitivities without pandering to petty idiosyncrasies. It is pre-supposed that leaders must develop or affirm (personally, professionally, and organizationally) explicit ethical frameworks in order to proceed with integrity in the stewardship of their tasks and relationships.

It is my contention that in some ways we need more "ethical fanatics" in the organizational world. Let me explain. In the negative sense, ethical fanatics might be described as leaders who, having lost their sense of direction and purpose, cope by doubling their speed. I would want to stay clear of such an individual. On the other hand, I think that we need thoughtful and conscience-driven servant leaders who are willing to take some "personal hits" for the sake of their own and their organization's integrity. Such people are fanatics in the sense that others may muse about or even belittle the energy that this person puts into ethical thinking and acting. But this is the kind of person I'd like to serve with. Ethical heroes are needed every day in our organizations and institutions.

If it is true that most of us think that doing the right thing is more costly than it really is, and that we often underestimate the cost of failing to do the right thing, this should give us pause. Remember that we typically judge others' worst actions by our own best intentions. Obviously this is not a fair comparison. Only the ethically discerning person can see the ethical imperative of an authentic ethical do gooder.

It is true that bad ethics is always bad leadership. Poor ethics perpetuate more

bad ethics and generate more policy and regulations. Shouldn't we work to be more discerning? All of us will have experience

that helps us affirm the notion that poor ethics creates suspicion, anxiety, and loss of control—and causes the degeneration of trust. Our research unit currently has no less than six studies of trust going now; it is an extremely important leader concept, a complex and fragile condition in any organization.

Accounting for these factors argues for giving much impor- tance—perhaps even being fanatical—about

> *A key characteristic of servanthood is humility.*

one's own and one's organization's ethics. Discernment sees this larger picture but also consists of the capacity to pick up the ethical nuances of situations and circumstances. Discernment will not allow a blind eye to be turned to situations that threaten ethical integrity.

Ethical Determination

These are precarious and perilous times indeed. One only needs to open a newspaper in today's cynical environment to see that leaders' conduct is commonly construed in the worst possible light. In general, public leaders are often presumed guilty of ethical offense by consensual validation that has no resemblance to fair process or substantive grounds. There are some "bad egg" leaders in recent times, ones who make it difficult (reputation-wise) for all of us.

At an extreme, all officials within private, public, and social sectors tend to be considered unfairly as being no better than the worst of their number. The same is true of at least some professions—for example, accountancy and law. The ungracious brunt of jokes and tarring by broad brush generalizations has transformed the noble into the scorned. Undeserved imputations and unjust malignment must be counted by servant leaders to show a scoundrel-weary age that, for the most part, the skeptics are in error.

Ethics in the Marketplace

The marketplace for professional services, whether legal, public service, health care, or education, need not be brutal. However, as economies, technologies, systems, and structures change, and as opportunism comes to characterize many attitudes throughout society and within these fields, we need to be aware and wary of the reductionist ethics of those around us.

Most of us are associated with organizations, businesses, movements, institutions, or groups who have been seen as 'great arenas of ethical excitement.' We all appreciate the pervasive nature of ethics in the work we do as servant leaders. As I suggested earlier, virtually every significant decision made by leaders has some ethical qualities associated with it. Perhaps all decisions related to people and relationships are inherently ethical decisions. They are not just ethical decisions in isolation—they may be organizational, administrative, political, legal, social, or spiritual—but we can be certain that there are ethical implications and ramifications with each of these decisions in terms of motivation, action, obligations, and consequences.

> A "lone servant leader" is a contradiction in terms.

I think the determination of ethical pathways is made more difficult with some conceptual mistakes or myths that need to be corrected. For example:

> Some say that ethics and the law are the same thing.
> Some are convinced that ethics are a personal thing.
> We have all heard people perpetuate the myth that ethical character is fixed at an early age.
> I have heard speakers who think that people who do no moral wrong are ethical.
> There are even some who believe that

acting and being ethical are easy for us.

The well-armed and reflective servant leader needs to challenge each of these statements, recognizing how subtly they make their ways into the minds and hearts of women and men in their organizational settings.

Such unfounded statements need to be displaced with more rigorous and balanced understandings.

What Is Ethics About?

Ethics is not about rhetoric—what we say, what we intend, what is written, or what we have framed into a credo. Rather, ethics is about actions and attitudes, who we are as people, how we treat people, who we are when no one seems to be looking. It is about choosing to do more than the law requires and less than the law allows.

Ethics is not about compliance, but about doing what is right, good, just, virtuous, and proper. It is not about the way things are, but about how they ought to be. Ethics is a set of principles that guide our attitudes, choices, and actions. Ethics for us, and the people we serve or whose interests we look out for, is about being, in reality, the kind of person we want others to think we are when we are at our best. Our best is consistent with externally-derived principles of obligation, ends, motive, and virtue that distinguish for us how we should determine right from wrong, good from bad, proper from improper, and virtuous from vicious. Ethics has two aspects:

> the ability to discern right from wrong, good from evil, ethical from unethical
>
> the commitment and courage to dowhat is right, good and ethical— while declining to do the wrong, evil,

or unethical

Ethics and Values

Ethics and values are not the same. Nor are they interchangeable terms. They need to be seen as two sides of the same coin:

Values are the important beliefs, desires, and preferences that shape our attitudes and motivate our actions.

Ethics are a sub-set of values, but refer to core principles which determine right and wrong, good and bad, virtuous and vicious, righteous and sinful (i.e., honesty, promise keeping, respect, caring, etc.)

We are all different, and values vary greatly between people. In this sense, diversity and "different strokes for different folks" may be fine; but when it comes to ethics, the content is more stable, and consensus is much more achievable. It may be said that true servant leaders manage or mediate values but affirm, stand for and by, and influence others with ethics.

Ethical principles are universal and, when not in conflict with other ethical principles, should "trump," or over-ride, neutral, religious, or cultural values.

Ethical Deliberation

As servant leaders, we must work consciously for continuous improvement in our ethical behaviour and be examples to others. Within all the diversity that surrounds us, we must have, prescribe, and live by a clear set of ethics—the tools which will allow us to mediate and manage values, processes, and content—for ourselves and those who look to us for leadership.

This is a path which we must tread with great sensitivity. The story has been recounted of a meeting of college educators at Harvard University about 20 years ago. At one of the open forums associated with this meeting, Frank Rhodes, the president of Cornell University, suggested to his audience that it was time for educational institutions to pay "real and sustained attention to students' intellectual and moral well-being," as these institutions work to reform themselves.

There were gasps from the audience, according to reports, with one angry student standing to demand indignantly "Who is going to do the instructing? Whose morality are we going to follow?"

The audience apparently affirmed the interrupter with loud applause, as if to suggest that he had posed an unanswerable question. President Rhodes, we are told, sat down, either unable or perhaps unwilling to respond. The question seems a most appropriate one to ask of leaders: "Whose morality are we going to espouse?"

Perhaps every person who would be a servant leader, whether a human services professional, business person, educator, politician, or public administrator ought to put him or herself in President Rhodes' position, by asking "What would my response have been?"

> We need to build discerning professional learning communities, with people of conscience and critique, commitment and covenant.

Inhibiting Factors in Ethical Leadership

I think a number of rationalizations keep us from our best ethical thinking. If a rationalization is an attempt of the human mind to persuade the human spirit or heart to change its position on a given issue or issues, then most of us will be able to relate to the understanding that we are sometimes "walking civil wars." The contests of head and heart in ethical deliberation can be significant for us. This is especially so in a pluralistic society. However, it is not necessary to "ship one's mind to the Arctic" in order to work out some of these conflicts. In fact, rationalizations are rarely grounded in substantive arguments. Typically, Pascal was right in suggesting that "the heart has reasons that reason knows not of."

Below, I suggest a few examples of rationalizations which get in the way of cleaner and clearer ethical deliberation. These are rationalizations that we should recognize and avoid:

Ethical agnosticism. This says to us that we can never know what the ethical action or attitude is—so why bother to be deliberate?

Ethical cynicism. This asks us the question, "What does it matter—do you really think it is going to make any difference doing right or wrong?"

The doctrine of "relative filth." This tells us that a particular policy or decision may be wrong but it is justified by the possibility that others are doing worse.

The jam of "false necessity." This explains to our hearts that we have no other choice, that there is no escaping the tragic dilemma we are facing.

Statistical morality. This tells us that it may be unethical to do something but it is legitimated by the fact that everybody else is doing it—or may be soon—so why be last?

Of course, there are many other forms of ethical rationalization, but these examples serve to demonstrate how commonplace and subtle they are.

We would all agree that obvious wrongdoing such as violating laws, rules, or acts involving dishonesty or

> It is true that bad ethics is always bad leadership.

disregard for ethical standards will get us into trouble. We may be somewhat less convinced that the appearance of wrongdoing is unethical—where we engage in conduct that is likely to generate or reinforce cynical attitudes and suspicions about our organizations and the people who lead and manage these enterprises.

These general rationalizations can be accompanied by other subtle enemies of integrity, such as: careerism; naive relativism, short-term thinking; the arrogance of power; independence; misplaced loyalty; egoism; carelessness; neglect; unforgiveness; obduracy; and otherwise crooked thinking.

We must not grow weary along the way. Again, we live in a precarious age. It is an uphill battle, right from the start, to be, and to be seen as, an ethical servant leader—somebody who serves others with integrity. Metaphors for standing strong in the wind or storms abound: roots, foundations, and anchors come to mind.

Simply on the basis of the fact of your leadership position, unthinking people will brand you as "unethical." "How did that person get there?" they will say, or "They must have done something wrong to get through the system to this position." As we know, servant leadership is first about serving, not about positionality.

As I have said, people are judged by their worst acts, with no regard to their best intentions, much less their most noble acts. Often we are judged by our last, worst act. Inconsistency in ethics can be defined in a moment by one thoughtless gesture, word, or action. This is why we must diligently work to be ethical, act ethically, and appear to be ethical.

Ethical Diligence

Robert Coles, the eminent Harvard psychiatrist who has given us books such as the Pulitzer Prize-winning Children in Crisis, The Moral Life of Children, and so many other worthwhile writings, tells the story of a woman of colour, the mother of Ruby Bridges, who was one of the children in a study he was conducting.

Coles says that "she pointed out that 'there's a lot of people who talk about doing good, and a lot of people who always worry about whether they're doing right or doing wrong.' Finally there are some other folks: 'They just put their lives on the line for what's right, and they may not be the ones who talk a lot or argue a lot or worry a lot; they just do a lot!' "

Readers of this article may have read Peter Drucker's preface to the excellent book, *Leaders of the Future.* Drucker used as a title the phrase "Too Few Generals Were Killed." This captures some of the same ideas, intelligence, and wisdom expressed by Ruby Bridges' mother. Leaders need to be diligent, relentless, and courageous doers of ethics.

We all know the clichés about walking one's talk, but 'ethics is easier said than done.' Drucker was recalling that it is too often the case that we have everything worked out in our minds as leaders, but don't get into the trenches, roll up our sleeves and do the work (the work of ethical exercise, or wrestling with ethical issues and problems that confront us). This is our call to due diligence as servant leaders.

We must recall that ethics is not just "doing no wrong;" but it is also about "doing right." There are lots of reasons why we are not ethically active. We are constrained at different levels of concern (individual, organizational, professional, organization level, community level, societal level) and the further constraints of uncertainty, lack of ability, inadequate information, or analysis, legal conflicts, structural or procedural barriers, and so forth are not insignificant.

Many ethical problems are messy. Timing is important. There is a need to build our ethical acumen to sort through ethical conflicts: right versus wrong; good versus good; right versus bad; right versus inefficient, etc. As Peter Vaill once suggested, we need to be diligent in working through these tough decisions, reflectively, collectively, holistically, and spiritually. In organizations or institutions, we need to develop a team of people who can give attention to systemic and large problems through public discourse and the various instruments of dialogical and diagnostic competencies. These are not small problems—there are no quick fixes, no three-step decision triages, or templates to put the complex and sacred activities of your leadership through, to come up with actionable answers. In tough times, ethical issues can be complex, and the pressures to be merely technically sophisticated and instrumental, rather than fundamentally ethical, exert powerful influence on us.

> Discernment will not allow a blind eye to be turned to situations that threaten ethical integrity.

The people with whom we work, those who work for us, and those for whom we work, are walking civil wars, like you and I. We know what is right and what is wrong from an ethical perspective, and sometimes we lose the internal struggle to choose right. We know that happens, and we know it is going to happen. Pre-commitment to ethical principles is a great help to sustained ethical integrity. I recommend that people make the decision to be honest, promise keeping, caring, and respectful ahead of time—then they don't have to make the decision every time.

Diligent servant leaders do not grow weary in all their well-doing. They insist on the resolution of ethical issues and problems in a manner and fashion worthy of their professional and leadership callings.

Most of my research work is of an empirical-design to generate descriptions from ethical leaders (including trustees, chief executives, middle managers, directors, and public administrators) about what is ethical to them, what the problems are, and what the pressures, basis, grounds, and rationale for their decision-making might be.

This has created a huge pool of data with hundreds of interviews and thousands of survey pieces. It is likely that I have never personally worked with the specific organization where you do your working and leading. However, on the evidence of my experience in several other English-speaking countries, I know that almost all the leaders I have connected with are up to their ears in sensitive ethical issues, as a significant part of their day-to-day work. Those who say they are not, often seem to be in a state of absolute denial. Most want to deal with the issues—to be, do, and achieve the best that they can. They realize this will not happen unless they maintain their own integrity—the elements over which they have most control—and they work consciously to foster an ethical environment within their organizational settings.

> *Perhaps all decisions related to people and relationships are inherently ethical decisions.*

Harking to a guru in the leadership field, Warren Bennis says that if leaders fail, it is by virtue of their loss of character or competence in the eyes of those they serve. There is a loss of trust in the integrity of fallen or failing leaders.

For our international and national-level leaders, many issues and challenges are management ones; they have dollar signs attached to them. This is where they often feel the greatest threat with regard to their ethical decision-making. Beyond economic and efficiency issues, they list a range of interpersonal issues—everything from "I am dealing with incompetence," through significant human questions of equity, community, and individual liberty. My concern in this short essay has not been so much for these larger issues but for the issues and situations where we do exercise personal and professional choice and influence.

You need to know the "best interests of the people" you serve—a deep understanding of purposes, missions, core values, and processes that goes beyond rhetoric—and an abiding commitment to making it happen. As a leader, you make hundreds of decisions. All of the roles you assume as a leader need to be founded or rooted in some solid commitments: to common ethicalvalues; to the voice of professional convictions; to your personal conscience; and to your professional and social constraints (codes). From this core of ethical commitments, you can sustain the integral core of who you are (a person who has chosen to be ethical) through and into these roles, where conflicts are sure to come. Consistently displaying all these core commitments in each of the roles you take on as a leader is what integrity is all about.

Servant leadership is about making sure your ethical core permeates all you do, all you are, and all you dare to be as a person of integrity. I could say much more about all this but let me leave it there—and wish you well in your journey as a servant leader!

PERSONAL REFLECTION EXERCISE

In this article Keith Walker states that we don't have to be ethically sick or corrupt to get ethically better. Compose a list of what you might be doing better ethically.

Select a "wisdom figure" for whom you have tremendous ethical respect. Imagine you are having a conversation with him about your list of doing better ethically. What advice do you think this person would give you about your ethical improvement?

SMALL GROUP LEARNING TASKS

Form new small groups of four. Create an ethical rebuttal for each rationalization in Walker's article.

1. Ethical agnosticism. This says that we can never know what the ethical action or attitude is — so why bother to be deliberate?

2. Ethical cynicism. This asks us the question, "What does it matter — do you really think it is going to make any difference — doing right or wrong?"

3. The doctrine of "relative filth." This tells us that a particular policy or decision may be wrong but it is justified by the possibility that others are doing worse.

4. The jam of "false necessity." This explains to our hearts that we have no other choice — that there is no escaping the tragic dilemma we are facing.

5. Statistical morality. This tells us that it may be unethical to do something but it is legitimated by the fact that everybody else is doing it — or may be soon — so why be last?

We'll hear your rebuttals in the large group.

The Posture of a Servant Leader

by Tim Gibson

Summary: When it comes to walking among those we presume to serve, it is critical to assume a correct posture—that is, a learning, serving, and storytelling, posture.

One mark of a world class runner is correct posture. Without any notice of their speed, individuals who run well can be noted by the stance they take as they move down the track. Back when there was a greater emphasis by parents on the art of developing, square shoulders, a straight back, and a confident gait, children were encouraged to develop "correct posture" as well. In recent years, this emphasis has received less press, but good posture is still associated with personal effectiveness and good health. A healthy stance does not happen automatically; it comes about through the development of key muscles that keep the body upright. Individuals who train their bodies in this way will maintain good posture, while others will not. One important aspect of this is developing muscles in key areas that help hold the body erect.

Individuals who would practice servant leadership must develop a correct "posture," as well. This does not come by default, but must be developed through discipline and training. There are three main "muscles" one should develop to be seen as a servant leader. They are learning, serving and storytelling. This is not a new concept. It is one that was utilized by Jesus 2000 years ago and one that is often part of communities that are oppressed.

In most cross-cultural situations, people often have the mistaken idea that they are to come across as confident, knowledgeable, and able to handle any situation. But when that posture is used, it often alienates the very people with whom you wish to build relationships. The concept of coming to a new situation as a learner who is open to the insight and understanding of others, rather than as one who has the answers and is looking for a question with which to use those answers, is more welcome in most cultures and in most situations.

> Individuals who would practice servant leadership must develop a correct "posture."

Tim Gibson, B.A., M.Div., serves as the executive director of World Servants International, a global partnership that focuses on transformational experiences for individuals and communities through providing short-term serving and learning opportunities. Tim has facilitated serving and learning experiences in the U.S. and in over 30 countries around the world.

Leadership and Learning

This muscle of learning is the first that needs to be developed. Learners use their eyes to observe what is happening around them. Learners also use their ears to hear what is going on around them. If learners use their mouth, it is usually to ask a question rather than to give an answer.

I once went to visit a community in Kenya, Africa, with our Kenyan director. The community wanted to build a church. After introductions were made, followed by about two hours of tea, cookies, and speeches, they began to address the concerns that brought us together. Our Kenyan director asked the local people how they intended to build their church. I became conscious that I was the only white person in the room as about 150 pairs of eyes were turned on me when the leader of the group said, "That is why we have invited our American friend." It was an interesting situation in which to find oneself. I felt like saying, "Of course, we will help." I also knew that if I did, I would undermine the authority and power of my Kenyan colleague.

What would a learner's response be in this situation? I had the capability of providing some of what they asked for, but what would I learn in that response and what would the community learn? I answered by saying that I didn't have the authority to make decisions regarding the plans of World Servants Kenya but that I was there to support the Kenyan director. There was a silence following that response that seemed like an eternity. Why was a white man deferring to a Kenyan woman? Aren't people from the West supposed to come with money? Don't you have the resources to provide? Aren't we the mission field and white people the missionaries?

Where are your resources when we need them?

Then our Kenyan director again asked, "So how do you intend to build your church?" After several minutes of silence, an older lady said that she knew of a banana plantation owner who might allow her to come and collect any bananas left after the harvesters went though the plantation. She would then sell those bananas in the market and give the money to the church for building. That started a three-hour conversation with almost everyone in the room coming up with a way that they could help with the building of the church. One man who operated heavy equipment for the government said the equipment was standing idle since elections were approaching. He was sure that, if

> *If learners use their mouth, it is usually to ask a question rather than to give an answer.*

he paid for the diesel fuel, his supervisor would let him use the equipment for excavating. In fact, his request was granted and for $60 worth of diesel fuel locals leveled the land and dug the foundation.

I received a letter from the pastor a few months later telling me that the church members now believed that they could complete the church themselves using local resources. He also invited us to bring a team to work alongside them to help finish the building sooner. This was a much different invitation than the first, which had World Servants providing the money for the construction of the church. Through our Kenyan director we accepted this invitation because now we were coming to work alongside people to assist them with their vision rather than paying for their vision to become reality.

I learned from reflecting on the situation that people often have local resources, but no one has helped them consider what those resources are and how they can be used. For our Kenyan office, there was a new awareness of the need for training communities in local resource development. In the next few years, the office taught more than 2000 pastors and community leaders how to identify and develop local resources.

> For our Kenyan office, there was a new awareness of the need for training communities in local resource development.

We later talked with the denominational leader of the church we assisted. He credited what happened in the church and community with a change of mindset that made the Kenyans see themselves as missionaries instead of a mission field. The people began to believe that they had resources, that it wasn't necessary to wait for the Westerner to come to make a difference in their community. While change like this takes years, it is amazing how one event can trigger a new way of thinking. In this case, it was seeing ourselves as learners rather than teachers.

Even learning another language is about putting another person in the place of a teacher and allowing them to teach us. For example, when you meet a person who speaks a language different than yours, after exchanging names, it is a good idea to place yourself immediately into the role of a learner by saying something like, "I am trying to learn your language." Frequently, I have seen this learner role break through barriers between people. It puts the other person in the role of teacher and lets him or her know you need help. A question such as, "What is this called?" gives dignity to another and opens the doorways of communication. It recognizes that you don't have all the answers and allows for exchange to take place.

A learning posture sees the process of learning as important as the learning itself and that discovery is more significant than getting the right answer. In working with people from different cultures, we have found that a significant way to assist them in the learning process is to help them reflect on their experience while creating shared experiences for the learners to reflect on together. Most of our deep learning is from reflecting on our life experiences and applying our discoveries to various situations in our lives.

Leadership and Reflection

The problem for a lot of people is that they are not encouraged to learn through reflection but rather to learn through intellectual development by going to school. The model they learn in institutions is one that gives them a theory, which they are then supposed to figure out how to use in real life. As I have talked with college graduates, I have found that in real life or on the job, they seldom use what they learned in their textbooks. Many study for their exams and as soon as the exam is over they forget what they studied because, essentially, they memorize it for the exam. In other words, they memorize what the teacher knows and recite it back to the teacher in a test so that they can get a good grade.

Reflection doesn't come naturally; rather, it is learned. When a person is a baby, the learning doesn't come from a book; it comes from trying something and discovering what it is about. Usually the baby has someone there who helps it reflect on what was just experienced so that the baby will understand what it's learning and know how to apply that learning the next time it's in a similar situation. For example, if a child touches a hot stove and receives a burn, a parent cares for the burn but also helps the child to realize that the stove is hot and will burn when touched. So you don't want to touch hot stoves unless you are willing to go through the pain of a burn. It doesn't usually matter how often you have told a child not to touch the hot stove, he or she will seldom believe it without experiencing the sensation of heat. If a child doesn't have an image of what a burn feels like, it will be hard for him or her to understand what the result of touching the stove will actually be.

As a follower of Jesus, I look at him as the ultimate servant leader. If you accept the fact that Jesus is the Son of God, then he could have come into our world in any form he chose. He could have come as a King and commanded his servants to obey him. He could have chosen many different forms of communicating who he was. After all, if he is God he has no limitations. But his choice was to come in the form of a baby. You can't get much more basic as a learner than a baby. A baby knows basically how to eat and eliminate. From that point on, they are learners. They learn from their parents, their extended family, their friends, their community, and their environment.

Jesus is basically not heard from for thirty years from the time of his birth to three years before his death. Why was God being silent all these years? I believe that Jesus was learning what it was like to be in human form and developing an understanding of all that we go through. He was a learner.

As I have read about other great leaders in history, much of their greatness is attributed to choices and actions developed from reflection on experiences they have had or observed and applying that learning to a new situation. A fundamental belief of a learner is: "I can learn from anyone and in any situation or experience."

This approach to learning is summarized in the following Learning Cycle. Many people have experiences in life and often do not reflect on those experiences. They just react to them, thus wasting the learning potential that was in the experience. People often need assistance in reflecting on their experiences. Part of that is related to the pace of our society and the dulling of our senses via media and entertainment that fills the space needed for reflection. When we help people create space in their lives for reflection, most can discover from their own experience the lessons that can be practically applied to their life circumstances.

The learning cycle demonstrates a way to take learning from experience and apply it to life. In reflecting on our experiences, we need to ask the descriptive questions so that we know what really took place and if we are interpreting it correctly. These are questions such as, "What did you do?" "What happened?" "What did you observe?" and "What did you feel?"

From description, one needs to be able to state what has been learned or is being learned. The best way to say this is, "I learned…" or "I am learning…" Once learning is articulated, one moves to action or application: "How will I use this learning in my life situation?" This model moves from practice or experience to theory or application.

Leadership and Serving

The second muscle to be developed in the posture of a servant leader is the actual action of serving. I hear a lot of people talk about being a servant leader but often speculate that those talking about it aren't doing much serving. For some, it is a style of leadership used to get others to do what you want. But it needs to be a lifestyle rather than just a style of leadership. A true servant leader serves. Servanthood becomes the foundation from which a person leads. Often those who claim servant leadership struggle with actually living it out. This is common since it seems contrary to what we think we de-

> The people began to believe that they had resources, that it wasn't necessary to wait for the Westerner to come to make a difference.

serve. A servant is one who comes alongside another not to impose a personal agenda but to assist and enable that individual to accomplish his or her vision. A true servant is one who serves even when others expect him or her to serve and when there is no recognition of the service: in other words, when it is not the choice of the one serving.

Many people at the grassroots of a community do not identify themselves as leaders because they have a view of leadership that is more of the directive approach. When asked what they do, they talk about how they serve each other and the community. One of the first things to do when assisting grassroots leaders is to help them identify who they serve and to realize they are actually being leaders in their community by serving. A leader is one who takes action to make a difference. A foundational belief for a person who wants to serve others is a firm belief that every person can make a difference. In other words, every person can be a servant leader.

> *Most of our deep learning is from reflecting on our life experiences and applying our discoveries.*

As I read the Bible, the people I identify as "great leaders" usually self-define themselves as servants. Moses, Abraham, Esther, David, Paul, James, and Jesus define themselves as servants. Their objective is to serve their master or their community.

When the mother of two of Jesus' closest followers asked for privileged positions for her two boys, Jesus responded by saying, "You have no idea what you're asking. Are you capable of drinking the cup that I'm about to drink?" The arrogant answer came back, "Sure why not?" When the other ten of Jesus' twelve closest followers heard about this request, they became angry—upset no doubt that their mothers hadn't asked the question first. So Jesus got them together to set things straight. He said, "You've observed how godless rulers throw their weight around, how quickly a little power goes to their heads. It's not going to be that way with you. Whoever wants to be great must become a servant. Whoever wants to be first among you must be your slave. That is what the Son of Man has done: He came to serve, not be served—and then to give away his life in exchange for the many who are held hostage." Later in that same story, Jesus tells his followers that if he has done this for them, then they are to follow his example and do it for others. In other words, they were to think and act contrary to the prevailing view of society.

In another story, Jesus and his disciples are about to eat a meal together. But there is no designated foot washer, the one who traditionally washes the feet of the dinner guests. I sometimes wonder if the attitude around the table wasn't something like this: Peter says, "Well, don't expect me to wash these dirty feet. After all, I am one of the closest to Jesus." James and John had just been speculating on who would sit at Jesus' side in his Kingdom so it certainly wouldn't be them. And the feelings must have been mutual for all the others because no one volunteered to wash the feet of those around the table.

The Book of John says that Jesus, knowing who he was and aware of his own power and authority, decided to "show them the full extent of his love. So he got up from the meal, took off his outer clothing, and wrapped a towel around his waist. After that, he poured water into a basin and began to wash his disciples' feet, drying them with the towel that was wrapped around him."

One of the key things to notice here is that Jesus made no distinction about who the people were or what he knew of their future actions. He knew that eventually Peter would deny ever knowing him, but he still washed his feet. He knew that Judas had already sold him out, but he still washed his feet. Jesus' serving them was not dependent on what they did with that serving act but rather on his desire and action to serve those he loved. Jesus' love took action. The full extent of his love was serving them and giving himself for them.

The acts of service Jesus did were the most ordinary and everyday tasks. He used towels, dishes, sandals, and all the other ordinary things of life to reveal what we are made of. He told stories about sheep and about lost coins, about sons and daughters, mothers and fathers, to powerfully give those listening a chance to reflect on their own lives. Suffice it to say that Jesus took the common themes of life to illustrate that his new form of leadership was very different from what they were used to in their culture.

Do you find yourself saying, "Oh, once I am in a leadership position I will be a servant"? The character that we demonstrate in our present life situation is an indicator of how we will act in other situations. Oftentimes people don't see that the way they handle the small things in life will dictate how they handle larger issues. If I am not a servant in my present setting, what makes me think I will be a servant when I get into a leadership position?

One of the most exciting things to local community leaders is seeing that the serving they are doing in their community is actually leading others to be involved and to take action. As we have worked with local communities in the U.S. and other countries, we have often found that the people who get things accomplished in their communities are not the official or appointed leaders but folks on the local level who define themselves as servants rather than leaders. When we help them see that others are following them, they are almost surprised. But they do begin to see themselves as leaders as well as servants.

The servant leader approach is often messy and usually slower than other approaches to leadership. It means finding out what serving another looks like from another's perspective. A servant uses his or her hands and feet to make the service practical. One must be present in the middle of the community to be able to serve. The one serving is striving to understand those that he or she is serving, which means using the tools of the learner—the eyes and ears—and combining those with the tools of serving—the hands and feet.

It is in the serving that one learns the practical lessons of life. Serving provides the experience for reflection, learning, and application. It is also in serving or giving of oneself that one experiences joy. Serving brings learning from practice to theory and, as such, is the bedrock for most community leadership development.

In *The Pedagogy of the Oppressed*, Paulo Freire, a Brazilian writer and Sixties activist, wrote that "only the power that springs from the weakness of the oppressed will be sufficiently strong to free both the oppressed and the oppressor." Freedom actually comes when one is served and given the choice to do what one will with that act of service. When Jesus offers his life as the way to an intimate relationship with God, he serves as the oppressed one. Those who seemingly have power to take his life, ultimately discover that their power is elusive, short-lived, and very limited. Yet the act of service that Jesus performs is an action that is taken

> *Reflection doesn't come naturally; rather, it is learned.*

without any restrictions on who can access the benefits of his service. Each person is free to choose what to do with this act of service.

So it must be with service to another human being. That serving must not be based on the choices or actions of the beneficiary but rather on the love in action of the one serving. It should be based on what the server is doing on behalf of the one served rather than whether the one served takes action on the service or even notices the service. The hardest time to be a servant is when no one recognizes that you are serving.

Leadership and Storytelling

The third muscle in the posture of a servant leader is that of storytelling. Everyone has a story to tell. This muscle depends on the other two muscles being developed. You are not likely to hear another's story, unless you have already demonstrated the posture of a learner and a servant, and you certainly haven't earned the right to share your story without developing the skills that are common to learners and servants. You probably won't be encouraged to share your story if you approach others as a teacher, leader, or preacher. In storytelling, one utilizes the ears, heart, and mouth. The ears and heart are used to hear empathically the story of another, and the mouth and the heart to tell your own story.

Why was God being silent all these years?

To exercise the muscle of a storyteller takes patience, empathy, courage, and vulnerability. It takes patience and empathy to listen to the story of another and really hear it. To really hear means that I will find things that I identify with and I will share that with the storyteller. I will also ask questions that make it clear that I heard their story, and I will affirm parts of their story that make me reflect on my own life. Once I have taken the time to listen to another's story, I will almost always be asked about my own story. It takes vulnerability and courage to honestly tell your own story.

One of the best ways to begin to tell your story is to put it into pictures that tell about your life. I have watched hundreds of people cut out pictures from magazines that represent significant events or moments of their lives and share them through tears and laughter with total strangers while deep bonds of friendship emerged. All of this can happen in less then one hour. Why is that? I think it's because in our culture, unless we have a spectacular story about our lives, we don't tend to share because we see ourselves as not having a story worth telling. But everyone has a story and when simple exercises are utilized to assist in the storytelling process, people are actually surprised at the depth of their stories. Add to that an empathic listener and an ordinary story takes on new meaning and power, even for the storyteller.

Again, if I look at the most famous storyteller of all times, I hear most of his communication with those he encounters in the form of story. Jesus used the common, everyday events, circumstances, and people around him to tell stories that we still hear today some 2000 years after he walked on this earth. He told stories about water, food, animals, kings, servants, girls, boys, men, women, fathers, sons, mothers, daughters, money, fields, harvest, sickness, death, life, boats, occupations, and the list goes on. Jesus seldom answers a question but rather tells a story and encourages the listeners to reflect on the story and come to their own conclusion. The question he often asks after telling a story like this might be paraphrased as, "What do you think?"

In working with people from other cultures, I have found that the posture of a learner, servant, and storyteller has led to deep personal friendships and allowed us to work together for the common good of a people and a community. Let me be a storyteller to help illustrate what I mean.

In the fall of 1999 I visited Kosovo with some friends soon after the war with the Serbs had come to an end and there was a peacekeeping force in place. I ate meals with new acquaintances, played with their children, met their families, and listened to their stories. Each time I listened to a story and shared my own feelings about the horror they had been through, I was asked about my family and what it was like where I lived. In other words, they wanted to hear my story as well. After spending two weeks with people in two communities, I asked what they were going to do now that the war was over. For many the answer was, "I don't know, but will you come back?" Over the next five years, World Servants took several teams of people to these two communities in Kosovo. Together with the community we built schools, clinics, community centers, and repaired homes. In the dedication of a clinic, the mayor of the city said these words that I will never forget: "We are thankful to the Americans and their God for building this clinic which will save thousands of lives. But we are even more grateful for their presence in our community which will be remembered for hundreds and hundreds of years."

When asked later about what he meant by his statement, he said something else, which now is ingrained in my mind and heart: "Money brings aid but people bring hope." He went on to explain how the relationships built sharing stories over a meal or coffee meant more than any building we could do. Money was impor-tant to provide for rebuilding our community but without hope the rebuilding is very empty, he told us. "What your teams did was provide encouragement and hope," he said. "It let our people know that other people cared about them and believed in them and our people responded."

An example of the people responding was when some volunteers from a church in the U.S. helped to clean up the sidewalks near an apartment building. At first there were only about five Americans digging up weeds and clearing debris. Soon there were as many as twenty children, most under the age of 13, who had shovels and hoes who were working together with the Americans. There was laughter and teasing and

> Often those who claim servant leadership struggle with actually living it out.

within a few hours several blocks had clean sidewalks, and children who were proud of their work! One of the fathers came out and, with tears in his eyes, thanked the team of volunteers. He said, "We have tried to get our kids to be hopeful, but it is hard because of what they have been through. However, when I looked out my window and saw all those children, including my own, laughing and smiling while they worked to make our community better, I became extremely grateful. You have produced a hope in these children and in me that no amount of money could ever do. This will be a story that we continue to tell to our children."

And it's a story that I will continue to tell because when you develop the posture and muscles of a servant leader, you have the

Quotes from the *Bible - New International Version* and *The Message*
Quote from *Pedagogy of the Oppressed* by Paulo Freire, Seabury Press, 1973

PERSONAL REFLECTION EXERCISE

1. Create a Collage of Your Life Story. Sit down with a few of your favorite magazines, a pair of scissors, glue and a poster size piece of paper. Cut out pictures from magazines that represent significant events of moments of your life that represent your life story. Bring your collage to class to share in your small group.

SMALL GROUP LEARNING TASK

Form pairs for this exercise that will take about an hour.

1. Each person has twenty-five minutes to share their collage and life story. The partner listening should focus on empathetic listening to the life story of his or her partner.

2. What did you learn from creating your collage and sharing it with another leader?

3. From this exercise what did you learn as a leader about the value of storytelling? List your discoveries on the chart provided. Appoint a spokesperson to share your discoveries on a Gallery Walk.

A Leadership Theory For The Commons of Alaska

by James Duncan

Summary: Based on a reading of Alaska's constitution, the theory of servant leadership has potential to work for the state of Alaska and other commonly managed states and countries.

In 1955 the Alaska State Constitutional Convention recognized the need to hold surface and subsurface resources commonly as an owner-state or commons. Governor Hickel refers to the state of Alaska as a ranch, and the executive branch of the state must manage like a foreman would manage the ranch.[1] The foreman must be a steward/trustee of all the resources so that the commons receives maximum benefit from its sustainable resources. In other words, the leader must have the beneficiaries' best interests in mind as he conducts the affairs of the state. Articles 1 and 8 speak to leadership that is holistic and working on the behalf of all the residents.

Article 1.

Section 1. Inherent Rights – This constitution is dedicated to the principles that all persons have a natural right to life, liberty, the pursuit of happiness, and the enjoyment of the rewards of their own industry;…that all persons have corresponding obligations to the people and to the State.

Section 2. Source of Government – All political power is inherent in the people. All government originates with the people, is founded upon their will only, and is instituted solely for the good of the people as a whole.

Article 8.

Section 1. Statement of Policy – It is the policy of the State to encourage the settlement of its land and the development of its resources by making them available for maximum use consistent with the public interest.

> Greenleaf takes his lead from Hermann Hesse's *Journey to the East.*

Section 2. General Authority – The legislature shall provide for the utilization, development, and conservation of all natural resources belonging to the State, including land and waters, for the maximumbenefit of its people.

Section 3. Common Use – Wherever occurring in their natural state, fish, wildlife, and waters are reserved to the people for common use.

James D. Duncan has been an Alaskan pastor for over 25 years. He graduated from Northwest University and is currently finishing a master's in education from Azusa Pacific University. Jim and his wife have traveled to over 20 different countries ministering in cross-cultural settings. Jim is involved in Alaska leadership as a presbyter and serves the state as a member of the Governor's Advisory Board on Alcohol and Drug Abuse.

Section 4. Sustained Yield – Fish, forests, wildlife, grasslands, and all other replenishable resources belonging to the State shall be utilized, developed, and maintained on the sustained yield principle, subject to preferences among beneficial uses.[2]

Just as the Constitutional Convention had to find a new way to fit Alaska's statehood bid, it is my hypothesis that we could search for a leadership theory that would fit the commons. This is certainly not the full answer to leadership for the commons, but I do believe—based on Constitutional wording such as for the good of the people as a whole, public interest, maximum benefit of its people, people for common use and subject to preferences among beneficial uses—that servant leadership deserves consideration as a theory for the commons.

> The words "servant" and "leader" are usually thought of as opposites by the corporate world.

As we open the door to discussion of what kind of leadership fits the commons, I will touch lightly on managerial, situational, transformational, hierarchical, and tribal leadership theory. The goal of this paper is not to draw specific parallels or comparisons. My goal is to explore servant leadership as a theory, discovering ways in which that theory could fit the state of Alaska, the state's Constitution, and other commonly managed states and countries. I hope that in the process of this journey, the reader can come to a conclusion of the best fit or theory for leadership in the commons.

Leading and Serving: An Important Combination

In a May 4, 1992, *Fortune* magazine article headlined, "The Leader as a Servant," Walter Kiechel III wrote, "…one can hardly visit the Temple of Corporate Heroes without running a substantial risk of being hit by a falling idol."[3] His example of Lee Iacocca of the late '80s has been far surpassed by the crash of Enron, Arthur Duncan, and Martha Stewart.[4] He goes on to explain, "…Perhaps the problem is not in our practice only, but in our theory as well. In the past several decades we have modeled transformational, visionary, autocratic, dictatorial, collaborative, situational, paternalistic, hierarchical, laissez-faire, democratic and sometimes flat-lined management."

In the 1960s Robert Greenleaf was the director of management research for AT&T. After retirement in 1964, he started a second career by launching the Center for Applied Ethics, a small think tank. Greenleaf began to study leadership models, and at the end of the '60s wrote and privately circulated an essay, "The Servant as Leader." Over the past twenty years, more than a quarter-million copies of the essay have been sold. Greenleaf takes his lead from Hermann Hesse's *Journey to the East*. In this book, the main character, Leo, does the lowliest of chores for a group of fellow travelers, but also buoys them with his good spirit and song. Leo is known as just a servant, but later the travelers find out that he is also the titular head of the sponsoring Order, a guiding spiritual leader, and a great and noble servant leader.

The words "servant" and "leader" are usually thought of as opposites by the corporate world. When opposites are brought together in a creative and meaningful way, a paradox emerges. Here, the words servant and leader have been brought together to create the paradoxical idea of servant leadership. The primary goal of the servant leader is to serve others, including employees, customers, and community. Servant leaders long to improve human conditions, offering hope and guidance for a new era in human development. This philosophy fits within the Alaska Constitution:

Article I. Section 1. Inherent Rights – This constitution is dedicated to the principles that all persons have a natural right to life, liberty, the pursuit of happiness, and the enjoyment of the rewards of their own industry....

The heart of Greenleaf's model is that by preferring others, the organization, institution, corporation, and leader will benefit. Nordstrom, the service-oriented clothing retailer, would be a corporate example. As employees show an aptitude for outstanding costumer service, they are promoted. Customer service, first and foremost, is at the core of the corporation's values.

Greenleaf believed that institutional structure was critical. "Too much of public concern for the quality of society is still devoted to caring directly for individuals and not enough attention goes to caring for institutions and the way they are structured," he wrote. "Caring for persons, the more able and the less able serving each other, is the rock upon which a good society is built. Whereas, until recently, caring was largely person to person, now most of it is mediated through institutions – often large, complex, powerful, impersonal, not always competent, and sometimes corrupt. If a better society is to be built, one that is more just and more loving, one that provides greater opportunity for its people, then the most open course is to raise both the capacity to serve and the very performance as servant of existing institutions by new regenerative forces operating within them."[5]

Leaders of the commons can see the parallels with words like "caring for persons...serving each other...greater opportunities for its people." In his own words, Greenleaf defines servant leadership as, "...servant first...it begins with the natural feeling that one wants to serve, to serve first and the best test of a servant leader is do the served grow as persons? Do they, while being served, become healthier, wiser, freer, more autonomous, more likely themselves to become servants? And what is the effect on the least privileged in society? Will they benefit or at least, not be further harmed?"[6]

Characteristics of Servant Leadership

Servant leadership has some of the same characteristics of other styles of leadership. I have chosen to highlight Listening and Foresight out of the ten key core values of Robert Greenleaf's teaching, synthesized by Larry Spears of the Greenleaf Center for Servant Leadership in Reflections of Leadership.[7] The remaining eight include Empathy, Healing, Awareness, Persuasion, Conceptualization, Stewardship, Commitment to the Growth of People, and Building Community. I purposefully refer to them as characteristics rather than skills. If the traits of servant leaders are intrinsically developed, then it would seem natural to refer to them as developed characteristics rather than traditionally learned skills. All of the ten characteristics can be learned and implemented. Greenleaf uses the language of leadership from a 30-year-old context. Over the last three decades, leadership has developed a whole new language. When necessary, I will change the language to fit today's context and the commons.

> The words "servant" and "leader" have been brought together to create the paradoxical idea of servant leadership.

1. Listening

Traditionally, leaders have been valued for their communication and decision-making skills. Servant leaders must reinforce these important skills by making a deep commitment to listening intently to others. Servant leaders seek to identify and clarify the will of a group such as the beneficiaries of the commons. They seek to listen receptively to what is being said and not being said. Listening also encompasses getting in touch with one's own inner voice and seeking to understand what one's body, spirit, and mind are communicating. Listening, coupled with regular periods of reflection, is essential to the growth of the servant leader.

In the commons, listening is conducted in public settings such as boards, commissions, and through public comment. It is also conducted in corporate settings and, particularly because of its culture, through tribal voice. Alaska's size and logistical challenges make listening imperative. The state has the most diverse landmass in the western hemisphere. What fits in Ketchikan will not work in Kotlik. The executive leaders of the commons need to hear from the local stewards of the land who know and have the state's best interests in mind.

A prime example is an experience that Governor Hickel had on St. Lawrence Island. One of the elders took him for a walk on the beach one evening. The governor commented on the lights of the boats from the local fishermen. The elder responded, "Governor, those lights you see out on the water tonight are not our fishermen. Those boats are factory trawlers and they belong to outside companies. They fish all the time, and we don't even know what's there."[8] This listening to the St. Lawrence Island elder led to CFQ's, (Community Fish Quotas) which return 7.5 percent of the profit from such outsiders back to the community where the resource originated.

A key element of the listening process also fits in the other characteristics, but serves the above illustration. Our Native/Eskimo community uses an "elder"

> *Servant leaders long to improve human conditions, offering hope and guidance for a new era of human development.*

system for leadership. This age-old, time-tested method of leadership is served by the core value of respect shown to elders. With respect, comes the critical element of listening to the elders. It is the way that these First Nation groups have transferred values from one generation to the next. If we are going to manage for a sustainable yield and do it with a mindset of benefiting all Alaskans, then doing it within the style of each region needs to be a core value. Subsistence lifestyle is not the only issue that could be enhanced by servant leadership listening. The state's education, judicial, infrastructure, social services, economy, and resource development efforts could benefit from the listening skills of the servant leader.

Listening skills also play a key role in Alaska as we attempt to build empathetic understanding and healing. In a state with 129 federally recognized tribes and more than 40 different languages spoken in one elementary school (Mt. View Elementary in Anchorage), listening becomes a key qualification for the leader of the commons. The servant leader should strive to develop an empathetic culture and assist in the healing process of cultural differences.

2. Foresight/Vision

The ability to foresee the likely outcome of a situation is hard to define, but easy to identify. One knows it when one sees it. Foresight is a characteristic that enables servant leaders to understand the lessons from the past, the realities of the present, and the likely consequence of a decision for the future. It is deeply rooted within the intuitive mind. Thus, foresight is the one servant leader characteristic with which some are born. All other characteristics can be consciously developed.

The leader of the Alaska Commons is well served by being defined as a visionary leader. Larry Spears says that foresight/

vision is intuitive and thus you are born with it.[9] I agree with Spears and also believe that a leader is not exempted from leading due to a lack of vision. A good leader can find trustworthy allies and perhaps staff to bolster their weaknesses. This is the most difficult area to staff due to the nature of vision. Finding visionary staff that a leader can trust takes time to develop. Trusting competent staff is also a strong servant leadership trait as the leader learns to empower those around him. In *Leadership That Works,* Leith Anderson says, "To admit lack of vision can be tantamount to abdicating leaders."[10] Most people who attain leadership roles are propelled by intrinsic motivation, which could be attributed to vision.

Here at the start of the twenty-first century, vision is being emphasized and popularized as never before. Even fast-food restaurants have vision statements posted on the walls. Vision has played a part of Alaska's development and can be seen through the eyes of men in search of gold, artists, explorers, mountain climbers, and, in the last 40 years, petroleum developers. Leaders of Alaska have also shown an extraordinary amount of vision to develop resources in a region so vast, varied, and sometimes unforgiving.

The key to all good visionary leadership is told by history and not by current barometers. Leaders are called upon not only to predict the future, but also to determine or dictate the future. The expectation is that leaders will be both prophets and kings. It is a high and unrealistic expectation, but it is the expectation nonetheless, making vision a particularly important leadership function, especially for the state of Alaska.

Vision in the commons should begin to answer the "why" question. Of the six great questions of life—"Who?" "What?" "Where?" "Why?" "When?" and "How?"—

"Why?" is the most important. The "Why?" question gives the organization or institution a reason for existence. Alaska's "why" for its leaders could be answered in Article 1, Section 1, which I addressed earlier. The second section of Article 1 says, "All government originates with the people, is founded upon their will only, and is instituted solely for the good of the people as a whole." I would draw from this that the primary purpose of a state leader is to always operate with what's best for the beneficiaries as a whole. If that is the leader's determined purpose, then out of that comes the vision statement. The vision statement should be easily memorized, explained, and understood. I would dare to suggest that an Alaskan leader's vision statement would read something such as: The Leadership office of Alaska exists to provide a lifestyle that all the beneficiaries as a whole can enjoy.

> The heart of Greenleaf's model is that by preferring others, the organization, institution, corporation, and leader will benefit.

Servant Leadership: An International Model

Servant leadership can be imported anywhere in the world due to the theory being made up of intrinsic character values. You can see the values surfacing in women who are willing to sacrifice for their children in Africa or the sisters at Mother Teresa's order in Calcutta. You also see it in those who are willing to serve at the risk of their own lives in Afghanistan and Iraq. The question is, can this model of the commons and servant leadership serve other countries, and, in particular, third world countries that have similarities with Alaska?

The leadership model of the Alaska Commons starts by recognizing the freedom of individuals in Article 1, Section 1.

"…persons have a natural right to life, liberty, the pursuit of happiness, and the enjoyment of the rewards of their own industry." Section 2 speaks to the leader's role. "All government originates with the people, is founded upon their will only, and is instituted solely for the good of the people as a whole."[11] The natural desire of people around the world is securing the freedom to choose their own destiny. Leadership that restricts, denies, inhibits, limits, suppresses, oppresses, obstructs, or frustrates is not leadership. The model of the commons calls leaders to seek the best for its beneficiaries.

> Over the last three decades, leadership has developed a whole new language.

How can a leader transition to servant leadership and help his or her country reach its full potential? The following bullets will help to navigate a country's new direction:

• Possess a deep guiding purpose: The leader must have the courage to explore a change. This includes changing culture, tradition, and even nepotism.

• Listen: Find the issues that followers are talking about.

• Get a clear vision: In order to chart a course, the leader will need to get a dream, idea, painting, or vision of what the change might look like.

• Gather a guiding coalition: Identify agents of change and begin to unleash trustworthy early-adapters who can partner with the leader's vision.

• Begin to paint the picture: The leader needs to communicate, at a catchable pace, what the transformation will look like. Communication would include how to attract producers, laborers, and other leaders.

• Track short-term wins: In the conceptualization, the leader needs to highlight short-term wins along the way. This will inspire individuals and corporate investors to believe in the future.

• Be open to beneficiaries, corporations, media, and other leaders: Being accountable keeps a leader on the right path. Change takes time, and along the way the leader will find many opportunities to be derailed. The leader cannot reject or avoid accountability.

The leader of the Alaska commons would need to look and listen, using vision and empathy, as he or she mediated Alaskans' inherent rights and their corresponding obligations. For the good of the people as a whole, this manager of the ranch would need all the resources of an enterpris-

NOTES

1 Name has been changed.

PERSONAL REFLECTION EXERCISE

1. In a democratic society each of us has opportunity to be a servant leader. Name one major issue facing society that seriously troubles you. Examine why by looking at the roots of that issue in your own life. Where did your concern begin? What will happen to society if it isn't addressed?

2. If you were a servant leader who could effect a change with that situation, what would be the key components of your strategy?

REFERENCES

Anderson, Leith. (1999). *Leadership That Works.* Minneapolis: Bethany House Publishers.

Barna, George. (Ed.). (1997). *Leaders on Leadership.* Ventura, CA: Regal Books

Blackaby, H., Blackaby, R. (2001). *Spiritual Leadership: Moving people on to God's agenda.* Nashville: Broadman & Holman.

Conger, J., Benjamin, B. (1999). *Building Leaders: How successful companies developed the next generation.* San Francisco: Jossey-Bass Inc.

Covey, Stephen. (1992). *Principle-Centered Leadership.* New York: Fireside.

Drucker, Peter. (1963-1994). *Peter Drucker on the Profession of Management.* Boston: Harvard Business School Publishing.

Ellis, Joseph. (2004). *His Excellency: George Washington.* New York: Alfred A. Knopf.

Hackman, M., Johnson, C. (2000). *Leadership: A communication perspective.* Prospect Heights: Waveland Press, Inc.

Hickel, Walter. (2002). *Crisis in Alaska: The Alaska Solution.* Oakland: Institute for Contemporary Studies.

Kotter, John. (1996). *Leading Change.* Boston: Harvard Business School Press.

Munroe, Myles. (1993). *Becoming a Leader.* Nassau: Pneuma Life Publishing.

Palmer, Parker. (1993). *To Know as We Are Known: A spirituality of education.* (2nd ed.). New York: HarperCollins Publishers.

Quinn, Robert. (1996). *Deep Change: Discovering the leader within.* San Francisco: John Wiley & Sons, Inc.

Rothman, Jay. (1997). *Resolving Identity-Based Conflicts in Nations, Organizations and Communities.* San Francisco: Jossey-Bass, Inc.

Spears, Larry. (Ed.). (1995). *Reflections on Leadership: How Robert Greenleaf's theory of servant leadership influenced today's top management thinkers.* New York: John Wiley & Sons, Inc.

NOTES

1 Walter J. Hickel, *Crisis in the Commons: The Alaska Solution.* (Oakland: Institute for Contemporary Studies, 2002), p. 81.

2 *The Constitution of the State of Alaska.* Ratified 1956. Produced by the Office of the Lieutenant Governor. Juneau, AK. 26

3 Walter Kiechel, "The Leader as a Servant," *Fortune* Magazine. May 4th 1992. Time Inc.

4 Robert Greenleaf, *The Servant as Leader.* (New York: Paulist Press, 1977), p. 45.

5 Greenleaf, p.13

6 Larry Spears, (Ed & Cm.), *Reflections on Leadership: How Robert Greenleaf's Theory of Servant Leadership Influenced Today's Top Management Thinkers.* (San Francisco: John Wiley & Sons, Inc), p. 4-7.

7 Hickel, p. 210.

8 Spears, p. 6.

9 Leith Anderson, *Leadership That Works.* (Minneapolis: Bethany House Publishers, 1999). p. 191.

10 *The Constitution of the State of Alaska.*

Authoritarian Versus Servant Leader Missionaries

by William N. Harris

Summary: In the context of cross-cultural church planting, authoritarian leadership is counter productive to the long term development of a church when compared to the Servant Leadership approach.

Introduction

When describing leadership approaches, one is quickly reduced to generalizations, though obviously no two leaders are alike even when they find themselves categorized identically. With apologies (in advance) for over-generalizing two classic categories, two leadership paradigms in contemporary missionary service stand in stark contrast to one another. One celebrates the tradition of authoritarianism in the form of paternalistic, ethnocentric, and foreign dominance, coupled with financial dependency on the missionary. I will contrast that approach with servant leadership.

Servant leadership is not a synonym for leadership by committee. It can be expressed across the full spectrum of leadership approaches, from autocratic to laissez-faire according to the contextual need. For example, a fleet admiral can be a servant leader as can a football coach, a country club host, or a leader who gives little guidance to subordinates who are able to perform well unsupervised. Servant leader-style missionaries can be found throughout that spectrum. Depending on the stage of the church plant, any of these approaches may be temporarily appropriate. However, missionary authoritarianism is about wielding power over others (however benevolently), whereas missionary servant leadership is about serving God by empowering others.

I argue that in the context of cross-cultural church planting, authoritarian leadership is counterproductive to the long-term development of a church when compared to the servant leadership approach. More effective are missionaries who support local Christian leaders from beneath rather than assuming lead positions themselves. They refuse to occupy any position that requires subsequent "turning over" or a "baton passing" phase. They avoid formal positions of unilateral authority (with the accompanying power to reward and punish) and watchfully avoid dependency-

William Harris lives in Siberia and serves as a career missionary with InterAct Ministries, mentoring Russian and Sakha church leaders. He holds three Masters degrees in the areas of Communications, Intercultural Studies and Leadership. He is fluent in Russian and has authored three books with a focus on American/Russian cultural differences. More information about his background and interests can be found at www.billandrobinharris.com

creating situations. This paper focuses on two leadership approaches I have observed in contemporary cross-cultural missions. Specifically, it compares missionary authoritarianism to servant leadership I have observed in Russia. I will describe the outcome of both paradigms and draw conclusions.

Authoritarian Versus Servant Leader Paradigms

According to Hackman & Johnson (2004), leadership approaches can be divided into three main categories: authoritarian, democratic, and laissez-faire. Of the three, authoritarianism most closely parallels paternalism. Authoritarianism "engages primarily in one-way, downward communication, controls discussion with followers, sets policy and procedures unilaterally, dominates interaction, personally directs the completion of tasks, rewards obedience and punishes mistakes, and exhibits poor listening skills" (p. 39). Domineering parents and paternalistic missionaries share all of these characteristics in common.

One reason pioneer church planting so often takes place with an authoritarian approach is that there are no existing leaders (initially) to disciple. By default, a missionary working alone can look to no one but himself or herself for leadership. Unfortunately, once the missionary begins in charge, the missionary tends to remain in charge. Authoritarian missionaries tend to grow dependent churches in permanent need of the missionary. When authoritarian missionaries leave the mission field, their churches often either collapse outright or dwindle significantly before undergoing a period of "shock" followed (perhaps) by gradual growth. Because they lead from above, authoritarian leaders struggle to turn over leadership to their unwilling followers.

Funding Field Projects

When it comes to creating and funding field projects (whether in the local church or community), paternalistic missionaries (and their authoritarian leaders) decide what to do, then "sell" those decisions to local believers. The result is expensive projects which photograph well but often are far beyond the resources of locals to maintain after the missionary departs. I knew of one authoritarian missionary who founded his church on foreign funding. After ten years, the church was still paying for 90 percent of its monthly expenses through the missionary. He built a congregation which could not survive without him.

In contrast, Mike Matthews (2001), the former Russia field director for InterAct Ministries said, "In InterAct, community development is done in the community, for the community, and by the community. …Community development projects should not generally have their 'birth' in the…[home] office of InterAct, nor in the mind of the InterAct recruiter, nor in some brainstorming session of an InterAct council." Note Matthew's focus on the issue of control. Who controls which projects are funded and pursued? Paternalism answers, "the missionary" (or sending mission agency) but servant leadership replies, "those whom we serve should initiate such projects." Of course, the missionary living in a community does, in some ways, include himself as a part of that community, at least as a newcomer learning the local culture. Matthews added that a missionary may "serve as a catalyst to move the community into discussing and acting upon some community development project. The project then begins (is given birth) not as an InterAct project or an individual missionary's project, but as a genuine community project."

Matthews did not mean that a project should be started by missionaries with the idea of transferring control to the community later on. Instead, he meant,

> *"from the beginning the local community has ownership. This means they more than just agree with the idea. It means they own the idea! It means the idea is theirs. It means the responsibility is theirs. It means the money is theirs. It means the initiative is theirs. It means the machinery is theirs. It means the planning is theirs. It means the debt is theirs. It means the success is theirs. It means the failure is theirs. It means — it means everything is theirs"* (Matthews, 2001).

Control Versus Decision by Consensus

A twisted rendering of the "golden rule" states that he who has the gold, makes the rules; money is a powerful way to control a church. This is especially true in missions, where foreign spending can easily overwhelm local resources. Proverbs 19:6 says, "Many curry favor with a ruler, and everyone is the friend of a man who gives gifts" (NIV). From watching missionaries' ministries, I know this to be true. The power of money opened many doors and headed off criticism of everyone on the payroll. One missionary I know enjoyed explosive growth in his church by showering financial resources on his fledgling church plant. At one point he had 26 of his 200 attendees employed by the church (i.e. by the missionary). Since over 90 percent of the church's income was generated by the missionary's foreign supporters, he felt it to be a matter of "good stewardship" to make all of the church's financial decisions unilaterally. Not surprisingly, when he fired all of them at once (hoping they would continue to serve but as volunteers), most of them

left the church, never to return. In short, money is power and authoritarian missionaries tend to use money in a controlling way. Servant leaders avoid control through money; they give with no strings attached and avoid creating dependency.

Another church I know well in Russia started with a minimal budget and no foreign funding. After ten years, its members not only fully paid for their own expenses but frequently gave generously to other churches in need. The servant leader style missionaries attending that church made a point to not give more significantly to the church than most other families. They could have given more, but did not want to condition the church to depend on them.

While authoritarian missionaries cover a wide range of personality styles (from heavy-handed to mild), they all share a willingness to control. When they form councils, the members advise the lone leader who then decides alone. Servant leaders also come in many personality styles but when designated as leaders, they decide by consensus, preferring a council of elders that grants each member one vote (the leader serving as first among equals).

Authoritarian missionary leaders assume control because they believe the best way to make sure work is accomplished is to take charge. In contrast, missionary servant leaders describe themselves not as leaders (who also serve), but as servants (who also lead). According to Mannoia (2005), the task of any servant leader is never to serve God's people (primarily). "There is a big difference between ministering to someone and being their servant....Leaders are called to serve one master, not many" (p. 57). The servant leader is not supposed to try to serve others by discovering their agendas and priorities, then trying to meet them. This would only pull him or her in multiple directions with frustratingly mixed priorities.

Such an effort would quickly destroy any leader. Rather, a servant leader missionary focuses on God's agendas and priorities, then compares requests for help to God's agendas and priorities and responds accordingly. Interestingly, even an accommodating missionary can assume an authoritarian role by accepting unilateral power at the local believers' insistence. Servant leader missionaries serve God alone, so they see their service in a church as a ministry to people on God's behalf (which sometimes means refusing people's requests).

The Servant Leader as Catalyst

In Russia where the authoritarian model is practiced throughout society in all sorts of organizations, evangelical churches tend to be very hierarchical with one strong male leader ruling with the support of a "brothers council" (similar to an elder board). New church plants initially are led by the lone missionary, but transition to brothers' council leadership. The healthiest churches decide matters within these brothers councils; the least healthy ones remain ruled by the pastor alone. Strong leaders who tend to dominate their brothers councils need good listening skills and humility to grow healthy churches. If the church has a strong leader who is willing to listen, good decisions can be made by a guided consensus.

The best foreign missionaries submit to the local leader and encourage the development of a brothers council. When they speak in those meetings they make it plain they are contributing their opinion, not making the decision. However, caution is advised, because the foreign missionary carries high status and can have undue influence.

Authoritarian missionaries readily act as leaders whereas servant leaders avoid accepting positions that can be filled by a local person. Instead, servant leaders act as catalysts, searching for a local person interested in a given job, then encouraging and assisting that person as needed.

Whether firm-handed or gentle, authoritarian missionaries generally accept invitations to lead. Servant leader missionaries generally refuse requests to take charge of anything a local person can lead. Unlike authoritarian leaders, they also avoid an activist role in business meetings and any other setting where they might (as foreigners) wield power to affect the outcome of a decision.

Discipling Through Scripture

A paternalistic church planter (even if very gentle) tends to be very relational, expecting obedience from his "spiritual children." While some missionaries take advantage of their special position, leveraging that affection toward control, others try to distance themselves from parent-child metaphors. In any case, those being discipled naturally pattern themselves after their mentors. According to Miller (2002),

> "The missionary plays a key role in showing them what they should change in their life. The missionary loves them and God and the new believers know and experience that truth. Their faith is established on their relationship with that missionary. They continue to grow and now become leaders in the Church, which looks quite strongly like any church from the missionaries sending culture."

Missionaries must be exceedingly careful to avoid unduly influencing new Christians on any basis other than scripture. In fact, servant leaders reject any authority but that of scripture (Mark 7:7). Occasionally, they are faced with questions from new believers like, "Pastor, now that I'm a Christian, should I keep living with my common-law husband?" Paternalistic missionaries either grant permission or forbid, believing it is their responsibility as spiritual parent to do so. Servant leader missionaries avoid pronouncing authoritative decisions. Instead, they may answer, "Let's look at the scriptures together. What do the scriptures directly teach about this?" Priest (1994) advises that missionaries not draw conclusions for others, but encourage them to exercise their own conscience. "[Missionaries] being from another culture…are the wrong persons to authoritatively address specific issues of lifestyle. They need to be humble enough to recognize this, and concerned enough about a healthy independent church that they refuse an inappropriate scope of authority" (p. 314).

When an American servant leader style missionary couple I know faced this situation, they found it helpful to direct people toward the scriptures and their conscience. For example, Yakut believers asked them, "Can we dance an okhokai [a slowly revolving circle dance] as a special worship expression? They replied, "Let's look together in the scriptures to see what God says." When they found nothing to criticize this, the missionaries then asked, "Have you searched your conscience? Will this harm your relationship with the Lord? What about your brothers and sisters in Christ? How will their relationship with you and with God be affected by your doing this?" Such questioning still did not reveal any problems, so with confidence, these believers went ahead, joyfully worshiping God using a form important to their culture. Following Priest's approach, they maintained respect for the consciences of believers by them to look to the Holy Spirit and scripture in directing their consciences (Hebrews 4:12).

Their ministry emphasized both public

and private encouragement, private correction, lots of confidential counseling, public support for the leaders, and some public teaching (never contradicting the leaders). If they had a doctrinal disagreement with a leader, they dealt with it privately (not always successfully, but always on the basis of scripture).

A Credible, Culturally-Sensitive Christian Witness

Missionaries depend on their financial supporters; prayer letters report progress to those supporters. That dynamic presses missionaries to show supporters the fruit of their efforts by filling their prayer letters with statistical data on the number of people they have personally converted, baptisms they have performed, copies they have distributed, villages they have visited, and so on; results validate their ministries. Servant leaders avoid the temptation to be too often photographed in prominent poses; they tend to stay behind the scenes, reporting ministry progress as a matter for prayer and celebration, but more humbly avoiding the temptation to strive for center stage (preserving that for Christ and local leaders instead).

When that same American servant leader-style missionary couple was assigned to assist Russian missionaries at the very beginning of a new church plant, they submitted to local leadership but also refused to assume some roles that they felt would have been counter-productive to accept. One of the Russian missionaries asked the American husband to preach every Sunday, but he only agreed to preach occasionally in order to avoid crowding out up-coming new Russian preachers in the congregation. Instead, he helped train those who wanted to preach, but wouldn't assist in baptisms because he wanted national converts to have a testimony that they were baptized by nationals, not foreigners.

Similarly, he made it clear that he preferred to see a Yakut believer lead another Yakut to Christ rather than do that himself. Their prayer letters would have been more impressive if he could boast of making converts, but he preferred to think of the future. Consider the powerful moment when a Yakut nonbeliever wants to dismiss Christianity as a foreign religion but his Yakut Christian friend replies, "No, it isn't foreign. I was led to Christ by another Yakut." The best role of the foreign missionary in evangelism is to provide a credible, culturally sensitive life witness, answer questions, even lead a non-Christian to the point of decision, then turn over the conversion moment to a trained Christian national.

Trusting God and the Indigenous Church

At its root, authoritarianism is based on fear within the leader. Fear and desire for control go together. The lower the trust, the higher the fear, and the greater the felt need to control. According to Kraft (1996), "The issues of power and paternalism are large ones, often rooted in lack of trust of the people we work with and, unconsciously, a lack of trust in God" (p. 407). Smalley (1996) added, "…Our paternalism is not only a paternalism toward the people to whom we go but a paternalism toward God. We regard the indigenous church as a complicated toy too difficult for God to handle" (p. 407).

In Russia, one of our most important roles as servant leader missionaries was to strengthen the local leader's walk with God, teaching them to depend on him for daily strength rather than leaning on us. It was a process that included counseling, Bible study, and prayer together. When leaders learn to trust God, their felt need to directly control events declines.

Exit Strategies, the Missionary as Scaffolding

Paternalistic church planters tend to structure their work with themselves at the center, like the center pole of a tent. Unless a similar pole can be found or made, the tent will collapse when the pole is removed. Designing a ministry with dependence on foreign-funding for church buildings, schools, guest houses, farms, bookstores, literature ministries, printing presses, wells, dams, aircraft, photocopy machines, water pumps, and electric generators virtually dooms a paternalistic church planter to permanent service (forever, if it was possible).

I have watched churches nose-dive after a paternalistic missionary left; no local person could fill the shoes of the foreign missionary. By nature, stronger authoritarian leaders tend to drive away other strong leaders rising up within their congregations, leaving only submissive followers who are ill-suited to replace the missionary leader later. For example, one church I know well was built around the personality of the beloved missionary who, basically, did everything. When he left, his congregation dispersed. When he returned, so did they.

A strong authoritarian missionary usually has great trouble convincing local believers to join him in leadership. Sometimes that is because he offers responsibility but micromanages the assigned leader. Other times, locals are too embarrassed by their shortcomings (well known by all) and feel ridiculous working alongside the all-knowing missionary. Their sermons attempts are not polished like his (though he patiently corrects them, trying to reshape them into his image), nor are their faults as easily overlooked by local people. I have witnessed local believers who deliberately "went on a drunk" just prior to the missionary's departure in order to disqualify themselves from the burden about to be heaped upon them.

Compare this to the servant leader's exit. From the very beginning, servant leaders see themselves not as tent center poles, but as scaffolding, a metaphor our mission's leaders have grown fond of. Scaffolding does not bear the weight of a structure, so when removed, nothing sags or falls. Servant leader missionaries are there to serve the local church leaders already in place. They take pains to avoid overshadowing novice Christian leaders and resist the temptation to correct them publicly. Undercutting a local leader is off-limits except under dire circumstances; even then, it should be should be done by locals. The missionary servant leader never turns anything over to local Christians because he has been careful to never accept responsibility for anything that might ever need to be turned over.

Holding the Door for Others

After six years as church planters in Russia, the American servant leader missionaries' departure from a successful new church plant amounted to a potluck goodbye party. There was no sag or stumble in the church that marked our exit. Coming alongside local leaders who were anxious to be helped made that clean exit possible. They were there to equip willing local leaders (who led right from the beginning), not to be leaders themselves who might eventually pass their baton on to others. Once local leaders showed from their handling of the scriptures that they understood how to interpret the Bible and could teach others to do likewise, the Americans stopped teaching that subject. They would refer people to those they knew could share that material clearly with others. They empowered others by giving away power, opening doors for others, and encouraging local

church leaders to let new believers serve who showed some interest in participating. They knew it was time to leave when the leaders showed they were consistently walking with God without need of assistance.

The servant leadership model does have significant weaknesses inherent to it (namely, that the servant's advice is not always followed when it should be). However, this is also a strength because the foreigner's counsel is not always sufficiently wise, and in any case, the fruitfulness of a servant model planted church far surpasses the foreign-dominated approach. Another weakness is that some worthwhile projects will never happen without foreign money. In those cases, at minimum, the missionaries should limit the downside of helping by avoiding projects which not only need foreign funds for start-up, but also ongoing maintenance.

Conclusion

It is tempting (and certainly easier) to lead by holding positional authority. It is frightening to stake the effectiveness of a ministry on the efforts of a carefully chosen team but that is what servant leaders do. Servant leaders show courage by refusing to control others, but the churches they help plant are healthier, more independent, more scripture and conscience-centered, and tend to reflect the local culture with less contamination by foreign influences.

My experience has been that the life example and overall ministry of servant leader missionaries promotes intimacy in these churches (since they have no unilateral rewarding/punishing role). I have also seen a spirit of servanthood permeate the church rather than members automatically looking to their leader to do everything. Most important, servant-led churches tend to grow more rapidly because more members are involved and assume leadership through brothers councils and other leadership opportunities. I believe that foreign missionaries who adopt the servant leader model will be rewarded for their efforts as they see those they serve reach maturity while helping others do the same. We are privileged to follow the example of Jesus, who emptied himself for us, serving us by denying himself, and even dying on our behalf. May God exalt himself through our ministries as we follow his example.

PERSONAL REFLECTION EXERCISE

Regardless of whether a leader works for a For Profit Corporation, an NGO or a FBO, control will always conflict with empowering others.

Describe your reaction whenever anyone – an institution, corporation, church, boss or spouse – makes decisions for you that you could best make for yourself.

In what situations do you become vulnerable to the need to control others?

What challenges will you face in directing your energies as leader to empowering instead of controlling others?

SMALL GROUP LEARNING TASKS

Form a new small group of four. Draw a Sunshine Wheel on the chart provided.

Draw a large circle with a small circle in the center. Write CONTROL in the center circle. Decide in your small group why we sometimes feel a need to control others. Appoint a spokesperson for your chart and post it on the blackboard or on a wall. After all groups have posted their charts we will have a "gallery walk" together to review them. Your spokesperson will explain your discoveries to the larger group as they walk by to observe your chart.

WHY PEOPLE TRY TO
CONTROL OTHERS

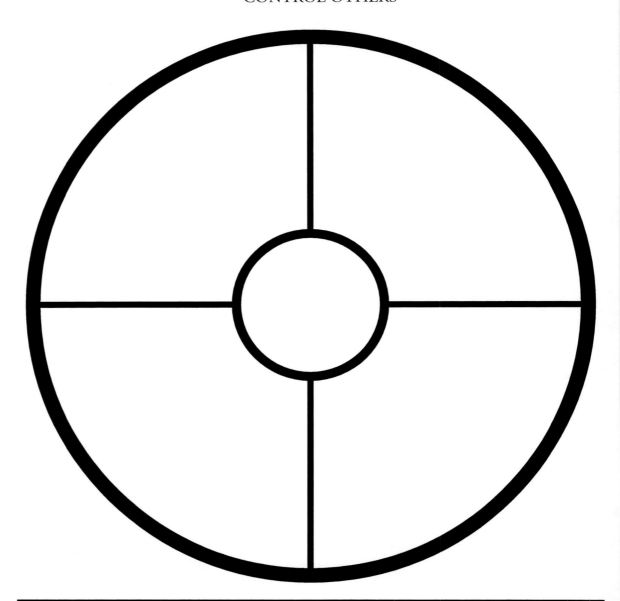

REFERENCES

Hackman, M. Z. & Johnson, C. E. (2004). *Leadership: A communication perspective (4th Ed.)*. Long Grove, IL: Waveland Press, Inc.

Kraft, C. H. (1996). *Anthropology for Christian witness*. Maryknoll, New York: Orbis Books.

Mannoia, K. W. (1997). *The integrity factor: A journey in leadership formation*. Indianapolis, IN: Light and Life Communications.

Matthews, M. (Nov. 13, 2001). *Personal communication.*

Miller, J. (May 6, 2002). *Personal communication.*

Priest, R. J. (July, 1994). *Missionary elenctics: Conscience and culture.* Missiology: An inter national review, Vol. XXII, No. 3.

Smalley, W. (1996). *Cited in Anthropology for Christian witness.* Maryknoll, New York: Orbis Books.

Servant Leadership —
A Needed Z-axis for Two-dimensional Leadership Thinking

by Bill Millard

Summary: True servant leadership is a mindset—a paradigm—that impacts every type of leadership style a leader may choose to adopt.

Leadership in the twenty-first century demands a different mindset. In the past, leadership in companies and organizations has often adopted a mindset that focused more on what was good for the leader than on what was good for those led. However, research now shows that these leaders may unknowingly have impeded productivity, effectiveness and efficiency in their organizations! Many of today's prominent new thinkers and writers in the area of leadership, such as Belasco, Blanchard, Covey, Garner, Kouzes, Peck, Peters, Posner, Senge, Spears, Stayer and Wheatly, agree upon and advocate the need to shift to a way of thinking that focuses more on leaders serving those who are led. In short, that is the concept of servant leadership. And servant leadership is the optimum mindset for twenty-first century leaders—

> Servant leadership is the optimum mindset for twenty-first century leaders.

whether they are leaders of large corporations or smaller, fast-paced entrepreneurial endeavors.

However, when the term "servant leadership" is heard, it often evokes somewhat negative reactions because servant leadership still remains a misunderstood concept. Recently I received a comment from a leader concerning the term "servant leadership" that I had used in a presentation. He suggested that the term was old and tired, and then he asked if there wasn't something more up-to-date and captivating. I have found this attitude shared by quite a few others in leadership and have been frustrated by the attitude. I have been trying to figure out what is fueling this type of reaction. The power of servant leadership has never been derived from terminology but from principle. Persons are compelled to be servant leaders because they believe it is the right way to lead, not because it is the latest

Bill Millard has researched, written, and spoken concerning servant leadership since the 1980s. He currently is the Executive Director of the Center for Life Calling and Leadership at Indiana Wesleyan University and an Associate Professor of Leadership. He earned his doctorate in Organizational Leadership from Pepperdine University. Bill has broad work experience in corporations, educational institutions, nonprofit organizations, small businesses and an entrepreneurial startup of two of his own companies, which he continues to oversee.

fad or the catchiest title in a pop-leadership culture.

Even though it has been more than three decades since Greenleaf first raised the concept in modern leadership discussion, there still is a misunderstanding of what servant leadership actually is. Many textbooks on leadership treat servant leadership more as a style than a mindset—and a less significant one which deserves little more than mention near the end. Others mistake it for a permissive and weak approach to leadership. Ask yourself, for example, what animal would you choose as the mascot for the University of Servant Leadership? If you are having difficulty with that mental exercise, try assessing the following situations:

Mary Smith, CEO of Acme Corporation, faces a serious dilemma. Her executive assistant continually shares confidential files with other people. Mary has spent several sessions listening to her assistant explain why he does this. She has explained to him why it cannot continue and has even had him meet with an outside counselor to help him work through this problem. Two days ago, the assistant shared a file with a peer. The company involved in the file discovered this and cancelled a ten million-dollar contract with Acme. Mary strives to lead Acme Corporation as a servant leader. As such, should she terminate the employee or should she continue seeking other remedies to help the employee overcome this problem?

Jim Green supervises the morning shift on a lawn mower assembly line for Farm Machines, Inc. Because of the danger involved with the product, strict guidelines must be followed to minimize accidents. Three new workers will start working on the assembly line today. None of them has any experience with an assembly line or with farm equipment. Jim will hold an orientation session with them for most of the morning. Jim conscientiously tries to maintain a servant leadership approach in supervising those working for him. Relying on this approach in the orientation session, should he primarily seek and listen to feedback from these new employees concerning how they think the assembly line should operate, or should he concentrate on providing them with directions on how to safely and efficiently operate the assembly line?

Paula Petersen takes her three-year-old daughter for a walk every morning. Today they are crossing a railroad track on the way to the park. The little girl finds the tracks fascinating and sits down on one of the rails. Just at this moment a train's horn sounds as it approaches from less than a quarter of a mile away. Paula believes that parenting forms the best place to practice servant leadership. Believing this, should Paula give her daughter time to talk about why she likes sitting on the rail, or should Paula grab the toddler off the tracks and escape the on-coming train?

> The power of servant leadership has never been derived from terminology but from principle.

True servant leadership is not a style that leaders choose to adopt only when they think it is appropriate. It is rather a mindset—a paradigm—that impacts every type of leadership style a leader may chose to adopt. But it is the muddling of leadership style and paradigm that has led to much of the confusion concerning servant leadership. This in part has been caused by the tendency of many who have written on the subject to concentrate on leadership behaviors—and equating behaviors with styles. But if servant leadership is a paradigm rather than a style, then the focus needs to be more on the mindset than on the specific behaviors (though these cannot be ignored).

Go back to the three situations just described. The solution to the third situation seems ridiculously easy to figure out. Your greatest act of service would be to save the life rather than to hold a therapy session. Use that same line of reasoning to examine the first two situations. Healing and restoration are important goals for a servant leader. However, the best service to all those who are led and to the organization in the first

> *Persons are compelled to be servant leaders because they believe it is the right way to lead.*

Servant-Leadership Paradigm

Copyright ©1997, 2000 Bill Millard, Ed.D.

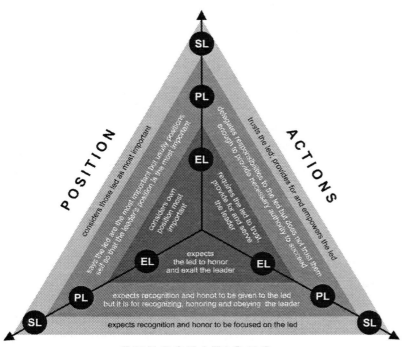

SL = Servant leaders focused first on those they lead
PL = Pseudo-servant leaders who often assume their focus is as servant leaders but who
   in practice exhibit a focus more like egocentric leaders (typifies most leaders)
EL = Egocentric leaders focused first on themselves

Figure 1. Servant Leadership Paradigm

situation is to terminate the executive assistant. He had gone beyond the ability of the CEO to bring about his healing and needs to face the consequences of continued wrong actions—actions from which the company needs to be protected. In the big-

ger picture, this is the best service and act of healing for the man involved as well. It gives him a better chance to learn and to change. In the second situation, feedback from those you lead forms an important source of information for the servant leader. However, the new employees' first day on a dangerous assembly line is not the right time. Life-protecting instructions are of far greater service to those led at this point.

Servant leadership, then, cannot always be equated with a passive, yielding behavior—the terms in which many think of it. I have joked that we need an article or book entitled "servant Leaders Can Kick Butt!" You can't concentrate on specific behaviors in understanding servant leadership because you will almost always be misled to examine those behaviors out of context. You have to focus more on the mindset of servant leadership, which keeps the greater picture of the situation as the context. The model shown in Figure 1 illustrates this by contrasting the mindset of servant leaders (leaders who focus first on those they lead) with what I will call egocentric leaders (leaders who focus first on themselves). The model compares the opposing leadership paradigms in three broad areas—position, actions, and expectations. The model also shows an intermediary mindset in leadership that is best described as patronizing leadership. These leaders often assume their focus is as servant leaders but in practice they exhibit a focus more like egocentric leaders. This probably typifies the majority of leaders.

As you look at the thinking pattern of a leader depicted in the inner triangle and compare it with the thinking of a leader depicted in the outer triangle, it becomes readily apparent that this is not just a matter of leadership style. This is a fundamental divergence of the way leaders think about themselves and those they lead. It is a paradigm. If you begin to understand servant leadership more as a paradigm rather than as a leadership style, you will find that its utility in leadership theory is greatly increased.

Laub (2003) articulated a three-fold contrast of leadership paradigms as well, only using categories of "autocratic" and "paternalistic" for the non-servant mindsets. I used that classification as well in earlier works. But I have concluded that it does not capture what we are really trying to convey in describing servant leadership as a paradigm. A case can be made that there is an appropriate place for a parental leadership style implied by the term "paternalistic." There may also be occasions when a leader has to act in an "autocratic" unilateral style. But even in these situations, there is never a place for either "ego-centric" or "patronizing" mindsets in good leadership.

If we understand servant leadership as a paradigm, it then becomes an overlay to other leadership models rather than a replacement of these models. In fact, I would like to suggest that servant leadership be considered as another dimension, a Z-axis, to all the various two-dimensional models of leadership.

Let me use Hersey and Blanchard's Situational Leadership Model as an example because it is widely used and is familiar to most leaders and managers. Figure 2 displays this model. The model is driven by a

Maturity of Followers scale at the bottom. This is a one-dimensional measurement of an independent variable ranging from immature followers on the right to mature followers on the left (maturity being a measure more of organizational or job maturity than of social maturity). This one-dimensional scale, however, interacts concurrently with a two-dimensional scale controlling the diagram above to determine a leadership style (dependent variable) based on the level of the maturity of the follower (independent variable). The X-axis on the upper scale, running from right to left, measures task behavior of the leader from high to low. The correlation on this scale is that the more immature the followers are, the more

> What animal would you choose as the mascot for the University of Servant Leadership?

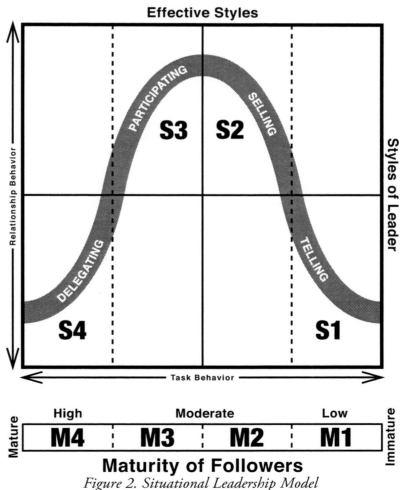

Effective Styles

Figure 2. Situational Leadership Model

task behavior the leader has to exhibit. The Y-axis, running from bottom to top, measures relationship behavior of the leader from low to high. Here the correlation is that at low and high maturity, the leader does not need to engage in highly relational behavior. But at moderate maturity this relationship behavior is required. The theory of this model is that a leader's effective style is based on the maturity of the followers which in turn determines the level of task and relationship behaviors, the two dimensions of the model, appropriate for the situation. *See Figure 2. Situational Leadership Model*

> *Healing and restoration are important goals for a servant leader.*

Whether or not you agree with this model, use it to understand what I am proposing with a Z-axis of servant leadership. Take the upper grid of this model and lay it flat (see Figure 3). The two dimensions of the model lie in a single plane.

Now superimpose a third dimension, a vertical axis, to that plane. This axis represents the paradigm of servant leadership. Rather than being another style added on to the four already identified by the Situational Leadership Model, the Z-axis controls how each of the styles will manifest itself based on the level of consistency with a servant leadership paradigm as described earlier. A "10" represents a true servant leader, and a "0" represents a pure egocentric leader. *See Figure 3. Applying the Z-Axis to Leadership Styles*

Look at S1 on the model. Here, the appropriate leadership style is identified as "telling" based on the low maturity of followers. But now take that "telling" up and down the servant leadership Z-axis. If the servant leadership mindset is low (0), the "telling" often manifests itself as "coercing" on the part of leaders where they intimidate those led with words in order to achieve their own way. If the servant leader-

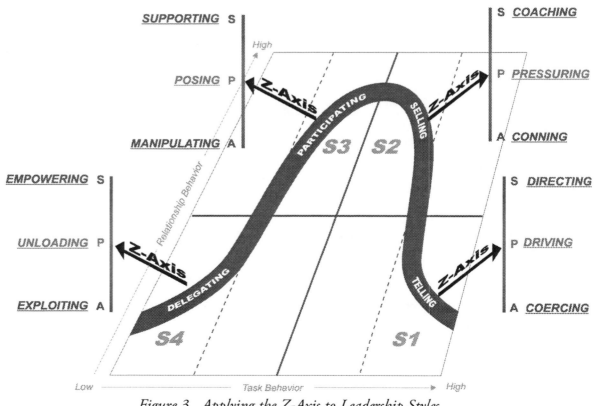

Figure 3. Applying the Z-Axis to Leadership Styles

ship mindset is high (10), the "telling" manifests itself as "directing" on the part of the leaders, arising from a desire by the leaders to guide those led in a way that is best for them and the organization. Patronizing leaders have a mindset somewhere between these two (5). They don't have the threatening intent to coerce; in fact, they often think they are directing. But in reality they carry out their leadership in a style best described as driving—as in a cowboy driving a herd of cattle because they think and act primarily focused on their own needs and interests rather than those of the led.

Move to S2 on the model. Here, the appropriate leadership style is identified as "selling," based on the somewhat-moderate maturity of followers. But now take that "selling" up and down the servant leadership Z-axis. If the servant leadership mindset is low (0), the "selling" often manifests itself as "conning" on the part of leaders who try to fool those led into carrying out the wishes of the leaders. If the servant leadership mindset is high (10), the "selling" manifests itself as "persuading" where leaders, out of true conviction, try to explain and convince the led as to what the leaders believe is best for the led and the organization. Patronizing leaders have a mindset somewhere between these two (5). They don't have the sly intent to con; in fact, they often think they are persuading. But in reality they carry out their leadership in a style best described as pressuring—as in the stereotypical view most of us have of a used-car salesperson. Again it is because they focus more on their own needs to show results than on the needs of the led.

Next, look at S3 on the model. Here the appropriate leadership style is identified as "participating," based on the fairly moderate maturity of followers. But now take that "participating" up and down the servant

leadership Z-axis. If the servant leadership mindset is low (0), the "participating" often manifests itself as "manipulating" on the part of leaders. In other words, make the led think you are one of them, and you can get them to do anything you want. If the servant leadership mindset is high (10), the "participating" manifests itself as "sharing" where leaders and the led truly work together in a spirit of community. Patronizing leaders have a mindset somewhere between these two (5). They don't have the hypocritical intent to manipulate; in fact, they often think they are sharing. But in reality they carry out their leadership in a style best described as posing—looking like they are part of the team when in reality they remain apart from any true sense of community. And this arises from their need to appear good to the led rather than understanding the need of the led to have the leader share in their community.

Finally, look at S4 on the model. Here the appropriate leadership style is identified as "delegating" based on the high maturity of followers. But now take that "delegating" up and down the servant leadership Z-axis. If the servant leadership mindset is low (0), the "delegating" often manifests itself as "exploiting" on the part of leaders where undesirable tasks are dumped on those led. If the servant leadership mindset is high (10), the "delegating" manifests itself as "empowering" where leaders turn over responsibility to those led, including the sharing of leadership, because the led are now capable and ready to assume such responsibility and will grow in the process. Patronizing leaders have a mindset somewhere between these two (5). They don't have the selfish intent to exploit; in fact, they often think they are empowering.

> *Servant leadership, then, cannot always be equated with a passive, yielding behavior—the terms in which many think of it.*

But in reality they carry out their leadership in a style best described as unloading—as in turning over unwanted work to the persons led with no thought as to whether or not these persons are the best ones to take it. This, too, results from a self-centered focus that asks, "How can I rid myself of some of my heavy load?" rather than "What can I give to the led that will best empower them in their efforts?"

It is interesting to note that Blanchard (2002) has changed his original terminology in later presentations of the Situational Leadership Model. He now terms the four areas as directing, coaching, supporting, and delegating.

What makes the difference in the paradigms? Let's revisit the leadership paradigm we looked at earlier in the triangle. This time let's summarize it in a chart, displaying three leadership choices, based on the mindset of leadership, and how this plays out in several areas (Figure 4):

Here is how Paradigms Matrix translates into the Z-axis. At the "0" levels on the Z-axis, leaders are more concerned about themselves and getting what is best for them. At the "5" levels on the Z-axis, the leaders may not have the overtly selfish "what is best for me" mindset, but they still primarily keep their leadership focus on the leader. At the "10" levels on the Z-axis, leaders are more concerned about what is best for the followers and goals of the organization. That basically defines the difference between servant and egocentric and/or patronizing leadership.

It is important to note that servant leadership does not supersede or eliminate the various styles in this leadership model. There is a time that requires a leadership style that tells, or sells, or participates, or delegates. But what is the intent when a leader, for instance, sells. It should be done

PARADIGMS OF LEADERSHIP MATRIX

	Egocentric	Patronizing	Servant
View of Leader	All-powerful	All-knowing	Steward
View of Followers	Primarily to serve the leader	Dependent on the leader's direction	Counterparts of leadership equation
Characterized by...	Dictatorial acts	Condescension	Mutual respect
Leader considers position a...	Throne for imposing edicts	Podium for imparting wisdom	Trust to faithfully carry out
Relation of Leader to Led	Upwardly isolated from led	Vertically elevated above led	Interconnected with led
Empowerment Flow	Demanded by leader from led to leader	Directed by leader from led to leader	Delegated by leader to led from leader
Responsibility	Hoarded by leader from led	Bestowed by leader on led	Shared by leader with led
Knowledge	Retained by leader	Dispensed by leader	Matrixed between leader and led
Communication	Quarantined	Monitored	Open
Response of Led to Leader	Fear and resentment	Resignation and compliance	Contagious synergy

Figure 4. Leadership Choices

with the purpose of persuading those led to see a better way to accomplish the goals, not to con them or defraud them or even drive them into providing for the selfish gains of the leader. The Z-axis, then, ensures that the two-dimensional model is carried out on the highest plane of true servant leadership principle. Such an approach is not restricted to the Situational Leadership Model alone. This Z-axis thinking can be applied to any valid leadership model.

In conclusion, let's return to that earlier comment concerning the out-datedness of servant leadership. Is that true? I don't believe so. What has become old and tired is the practice of looking at servant leadership as a soft and permissive style and its various behaviors as being the same in any situation—a style which is, frankly, ineffective. If, instead, servant leadership is seen as a paradigm in which a variety of leadership styles takes place, then it can also be seen as a vibrant and dynamic force that will bring about the kind of leadership advocated by so many in leadership theory today. A servant leadership paradigm will also form the foundation for ethics and character in leadership that is missing in many leadership arenas today.

PERSONAL REFLECTION EXERCISE

1. Identify a time when you had to deal with a very difficult problem at work that required assertive intervention. For example, Mary Smith should have fired an indiscreet employee, Jim Green needs forego prolonged relational pleasantries at the orientation meeting on how the assembly line should function for a new product, and Paula Peterson needs to swiftly pull her three year old off the rail-road tracks because of an oncoming train.

2. Being assertive is not easy and the outcome is not always pleasant. Assess how you handled the difficult situation that you identified. What factors make taking strong action easy or difficult for you? What servant leadership qualities can you further develop that will insure that when you do confront the hard things in the future, you do it with healthy respect for all involved.

SMALL GROUP LEARNING TASK

In small groups of three or four, read Marylen Black's story. Answer the questions that follow.

Marylen Black's Story

Marylen Black is an excellent professor who is highly competent in teaching and relational skills. She is teaching a graduate level class on servant leadership to NGO male leaders in Kenya. She quickly becomes aware that she is teaching in a male-dominant culture and that her students are skeptical about the effectiveness of servant leadership principles and Marylen's credentials to teach them. During a coffee break she overhears students complaining about her to each other.

What is happening here?

When it happens in your situation what problems will it cause?

According to the X and Y Axis, what kind of teaching style do you think Marylen needs to use?

If you were Marylen, what would you do?

REFERENCES

Blanchard, Ken. (2002). "Situational Leadership II."
    Available: http://www.kenblanchard.com/areas/situationalII.cfm

Laub, James A. (2004). "APS Model." Available:
    http://www.olagroup.com/concepts/aps_model.cfm

Developmental Issues in Servanthood:

Implications for Training and Development

by Ray Rood

Summary: The major developmental issues of the second half of life can be framed by questions concerning meaning and purpose and, ultimately, choosing to serve out of one's own identity.

As I prepared to write this article, I was struck by a conversation that I had within the last week with a women in her late thirties. During our conversation, she told me about her decision to terminate all of her church involvement except for occasional attendance. She went on to say that while she has been perceived as one of the most loyal, even ideal, church members, one who said "yes" to every need, she finally came to a place where she admitted to herself that her service was not a reflection of herself. Rather, it was a reflection of the values of her parents and the church of which she has always been a part. She believed it to be a turning point in her life when she announced to her minister that she would not be available any longer. As I listened to her story, I could not help but reflect on my own journey as a preacher's kid who was expected to be an example of giving and serving. I will never forget the messages, both formal and informal, against

> I could not help but reflect on my own journey as a preacher's kid who was expected to be an example of giving and serving.

self centeredness and my own historical battle against what a friend of mine called "the tyranny of the oughts and shoulds."

This conversation triggered thoughts about what could be called "service burnout." In numerous conversations over the past twenty years, I have heard similar descriptions of this burnout rendered by missionaries and church workers, many of whom believed they could only escape a de-energized servanthood through imagined and real illness that actually claimed lives. Reflecting on my conversation with this young woman triggered some other thoughts as well.

I can recall events and experiences where people of all ages, particularly younger people, got excited about helping others in need. I can remember a Christian service trip to Mexico with a group of high school students and the stories that were told about how lives were changed as a result of helping others who were less fortunate. I am also aware of countless stories of the meaning and purpose that emerged out of

Raymond Rood is president and senior consultant of Human Technologies International, a change management-consulting firm, and has consulted or taught in more than 30 countries. In his own words, he "helps organizations and individuals to dream and achieve great dreams."

volunteerism throughout this country and the world, where lives were enriched because somebody else gave willingly of his or her time, energy, and/or wealth.

As I reflect on these lives of service, a number of questions emerge for me. At least two of them carry special significance, namely:

When is giving service positive and when, if ever, is it negative?

How is servanthood related to the human development journey, and what is leadership's responsibilities in the involvement of others in service projects and events?

As a student of developmental psychology, I have been intrigued by the foundational work of Erik Erikson in developmental theory, particularly his Life Cycle of Man which was the first lifelong developmental model identified (presented at a symposium on the Healthy Personality in New York, 1950). Erikson, a Harvard professor and psychoanalyst, seemed to have an intuitive sense for the developmental tasks of life which he substantiated through research. He charted eight stages in the life cycle that are understood as the basic developmental issues in psycho-social development.

"Personality," Erikson has written, "can be said to develop according to steps predetermined in the human organism's readiness to be driven toward, to be aware of, and to interact with a widening social radius, beginning with a dim image of a mother and ending with an image of mankind. . ." Following are the steps he has identified in man's psycho-social development and the special crises they bring. In presenting them, he has emphasized that while the struggle between the negatives and positives in each crisis must be fought through successfully if the next developmental stage is to be reached, no victory is completely or forever won.

Infancy:
Trust vs. Mistrust

The first "task" of the infant is to develop "the cornerstone of healthy personality," a basic sense of trust—in himself and in his environment. This comes from a feeling of inner goodness derived from "the mutual regulation of his receptive capacities with the maternal techniques of provision"—a quality of care that transmits a sense of trustworthiness and meaning. The danger, most acute in the second half of the first year, is that discontinuities in care may increase a natural sense of loss, as the child gradually recognizes his separateness from his mother, to a basic sense of mistrust that may last through life.

Early Childhood:
Autonomy vs. Shame and Doubt

With muscular maturation, the child experiments with holding on and letting go and begins to attach enormous value to his autonomous will. The danger here is the development of a deep sense of shame and doubt if he is deprived of the opportunity to learn to develop his will as he learns his "duty," and therefore learns to expect defeat in any battle of wills with those who are bigger and stronger.

> The first "task" of the infant is to develop "the cornerstone of healthy personality," a basic sense of trust—in himself and in his environment.

Play Age:
Initiative vs. Guilt

In this stage, the child's imagination is greatly expanded because of his increased ability to move around freely and to communicate. It is an age of intrusive activity, avid curiosity, and consuming fantasies which lead to feelings of guilt and anxiety. It is also the stage of the establishment of conscience. If this tendency to feel guilty is "overburdened by all-too-eager adults" the child may develop a deep-seated conviction that he is essentially bad, with a resultant stifling of initiative or a conversion of his moralism to vindictiveness.

School Age:
Industry vs. Inferiority

The long period of sexual latency before puberty is the age when the child wants to learn how to do and make things with others. In learning to accept instruction and to win recognition by producing "things," he opens the way for the capacity of work employment. The danger of this period is the development of a sense of inadequacy and inferiority in a child who does not receive recognition for his efforts.

Adolescence:
Identity vs. Identify Diffusion

The physiological revolution that comes with puberty—rapid body growth and sexual maturity—forces the young person to question "all sameness and continuities relied on earlier" and to "re-fight many of the earlier battles." The developmental task is to integrate childhood identifications "with the basic biological drives, native endowments, and the opportunities offered in social roles." The danger is that identity diffusion, temporarily unavoidable in this period of physical and psychological upheaval, may result in a permanent inability to "take hold" of, because of youth's tendency to total commitment, in the fixation in the young person of a negative identity, a devoted attempt to become what parents, class, or community do not want him to be.

> A logical conclusion would be to look at the major developmental question of the first half of life as relating to the search for one's identity, or "Who am I?"

Young Adulthood:
Intimacy vs. Isolation

Only as a young person begins to feel more secure in his identity is he able to establish intimacy with himself (with his inner life) and with others, both in friendships and, eventually, in a love-based, mutually satisfying sexual relationship with a member of the opposite sex. A person who cannot enter wholly into an intimate relationship, because of the fear of losing his identity, may develop a deep sense of isolation.

Adulthood:
Generativity vs. Self-Absorption

Out of the intimacies of adulthood grows generativity—the mature person's interest in establishing and guiding the next generation. The lack of this results in self-absorption and, frequently, in a "pervading sense of stagnation and interpersonal impoverishment."

Mature Sdulthood:
Integrity vs. Despair

The person who has achieved a satisfying intimacy with other human beings and who has adapted to the triumphs and disappointments of his generative activities as parent and coworker reaches the end of life with a certain ego integrity—an acceptance of his own responsibilities for what his life is and was and of its place in the flow of history.

If Erikson was correct in his identification of the sequence of these life themes, then one conclusion would be that true and complete service is a high-level developmental task to be expressed naturally only by those in the second half of their lifetimes. Erikson's term "generativity," which means contributing to the well being of others, could serve as a developmental base or foundation for natural service which flows out of the essence of one's individual and unique identity—which in itself is a developmental task. A logical conclusion would be to look at the major developmental question of the first half of life as relating to the search for one's identity, or "Who am I?" Meanwhile, the second half of life would be framed by a question concerning the search for meaning and purpose, or "What am I going to do with 'who I am'?"

To the extent that this theory describes reality, it may be understandable why some individuals experience what I call "service burnout." An individual who has not developed a clear, integrated and unique sense of who one is may get involved in activities that are valued by those he or she values and thereby develop and solidify an identity and related self-esteem that is more external than internal. This identity can stay in place until it is meaningfully challenged by illness, a new and respected person outside one's historical milieu and/or one's own reflection, and self doubt. While such a challenge can emerge at any time, it often emerges during what has been called the "mid life transition," a transition which can result in dramatic, often conflict-related, behavioral changes. Such may be the case with the woman resigning from her church involvement. The tension in such a mid-life-related internal conversation is captured in the following Roy Clark song, "Right or Left at Oak Street":

The alarm rang at seven this morning
The same time it did yesterday.
Seven-thirty is my breakfast time,
And I know what the wife's going
to say.

Crawfords next door got a new
swimmin' pool,
The Millers'got a color T.V.
Mr. Wilson's job is not as good as
yours,
But his wife dresses better'n me.

I get to school at 8:05
And drop the kids off at the gate.
I drive past the clock outside the bank,
And it's exactly a quarter past eight.

When I reach the stop sign at
*   Oak Street*
The same thought crosses my mind:
Should I turn right as I always have
Or left and leave it all behind?

Right or left at Oak Street—
The choice I face every day.
And I don't know which takes more
*   courage…*
The stayin' or the runnin' away.

The challenge in these instances where a person makes a radical shift in behavior is that whatever symbolizes that which he or she is trying to free himself or herself from becomes a negative and may remain so up until one really determines who he or she is as opposed to who he or she is not.

> Research suggests that for most women, generativity is a continuous aspect of a female's life.

There is one other developmental variable that needs to be considered before we can consider the practical implications of training or developing servanthood within others. It was during the late seventies and early eighties that a new body of literature suggested that female development is distinctly different from male development in terms of process and how it unfolds. For example, female development involved negotiating developmental tasks on several fronts at once as opposed to male development which is characterized by a more linear, block-step series of transition and building stages. One specific difference that may be relevant to our discussion on servanthood is the developmental task of generativity. Research suggests that for most women, generativity is a continuous aspect of a female's life; it is a process much larger than reproduction, although childbearing and a desire to bear children are expressions of generativity for women. The importance of nurturing and taking care of permeates most females' life journey and is expressed in many creative ways throughout their lives, particularly the first half. This may explain why it is easier for most young women to make contributions to the lives of others compared to most young men.

> *It may be wise in the presentation of servanthood programs to present them not only as an opportunity to contribute but an opportunity to receive.*

One conclusion that seems to emerge out of this research suggests that there may be two developmental pathways to servanthood. The masculine pathway, which some women follow, according to the noted psychoanalyst Carl Jung, is a road towards identity that is an expression of what one does. On the other hand, the feminine pathway, which some men follow, says Jung, is a road where identity is more of an expression of with whom one is in relationship. What then are the implications for servanthood? Some of the possible answers include:

Initially, more young women will likely be drawn to serving than young men, although there will always be some exceptions where young men with an unusual amount of sensitivity will become involved. Leaders need to manage their expectations accordingly.

Female servanthood, for the most part, will be more instinctive, intuitive, and spontaneous. Meanwhile, most male servanthood will be more strategic and deliberate. Room needs to be made for both approaches.

More women may ask, "How can I contribute?" But more men may ask, "What will I receive out of my giving?" Both questions need to be encouraged.

It may be wise in the presentation of servanthood programs to present them not only as an opportunity to contribute but an opportunity to receive, including such benefits as learning and relating, which need to be described in meaningful ways.

The most important developmental implication of servanthood may well be the matter of choice. There seems a strong case for the importance of being able to choose to give as opposed to giving because one should, especially in light of the world's overwhelming needs. This is important for the mature person who gives out of his or her identity. It is important for the emerging adult who is moving from an external identity and the influence of the group to an internal and separate identify. Finally, it is important to consider the difference facing the young person who is overly influenced by "oughts," "shoulds" and group pressure. This is the kind of person who is most vulnerable to servant burnout where both the person and the needs of others suffer. In light of these things, it may be wise to encourage young people to be selective in their contributions, considering both who they are and who they are becoming. Encouraging them in this way will call for a full understanding of mature leadership and servanthood, especially on the part of those who support them in leadership. And it may be well for us all to remember that Jesus' ministry did not begin until he was thirty.

PERSONAL REFLECTION EXERCISE

From your own experience of serving and being served, answer these questions in the space below.

When is giving service positive?

When, if ever, is it negative?

SMALL GROUP LEARNING TASKS

Break up into small groups of three or four by gender – men only and women only. In your small group, make a chart of what service "looks like" to your gender. When you have completed your chart, appoint a spokesperson for your group. Post your chart on the wall, beside a chart from the opposite gender. Charts should be clustered in pairs around the room. After each pair has explained their charts, talk about what you have discovered by looking at them together.

REFERENCES

Erikson, E. H. (1968) *Identity: Youth and Crisis.* New York: WW Norton & Co.

Erikson, E.H. (1980) *Identity and the Life Cycle.* New York: WW Norton/ International University Press.

Gilligan C. (1977) *In a different voice: Women's conception of self and of morality.* Cambridge, MA: Harvard University Press.

Kegan, R. (1982) *The Evolving Self: Problem and process in human development.*

Sheehy, G. (1976) *Passages: Predictable Crises of Life.* New York E.P. Dutton.

The Servant Leadership Marriage:

Principles of Servant Leadership for Healthy Relationships and Marriages

by Kimberly Battle-Walters Denu

Summary: Healthy marriages aren't the product of chance but the daily practice of servan-tand sacrificial leadership.

"In every moment of life, we both lead and follow" — Dee Hock

Go to almost any American wedding and the tradition is that the bride and groom will throw the wedding bouquet and garter during their reception, as a symbolic gesture of foretelling the next bride to be. However nostalgic this ritual, I have recently come to believe that it would be more appropriate for couples to throw towels towards single guests during their reception, symbolizing the act of serving one another, as exemplified by Jesus in the washing of His disciples' feet, than flowers and garters. In the sacred vow marriage, there is no higher principle than servanthood.

Some have said that marriage is an institution. If so, a shift in thinking about marriage from the perspective of serving first, rather than approaching it primarily from a romantic side devoid of service, will hopefully alleviate some false expectations about marriage and return our focus to commitment instead. When looking for key elements in thriving and healthy marriages, one doesn't have to look much further than the principles of servant leadership that have been expressed by Robert Greenleaf and many others. Greenleaf's principle stresses the importance of seeking to serve first and foremost, rather than being served. In Western cultures, where the focus is nearly always a "What's in it for me?" mentality, it is no surprise that divorce rates are high and commitments are low. Serial monogamy—commitment to one relationship at a time, but no one relationship for life—has become a new model for many.

> In Western cultures, where the focus is nearly always a "What's in it for me?" mentality, it is no surprise that divorce rates are high and commitments are low.

The Servant Leadership Marriage

Applying Greenleaf's model to marriage, a servant leader(ship) marriage would be one where both partners focus on serving first and leading second, where there is a

Kimberly Battle-Walters Denu, Ph.D., is Professor of Social Work at Azusa Pacific University. She is also an ordained minister who has done ministry and service in the United States and six of the seven continents of the world. She was a Fulbright Scholar to South Africa and has published in the areas of ethnic, familial, and gender issues within global settings.

commitment to empowering each other and helping each other reach one's highest good, and where each partner leads by doing. The marriage works from the premise of a "team" leadership principle that encompasses a shared vision and mission/purpose statement for the marriage and the home. Although either partner will take the lead or responsibility for any given area in the marriage, both see their roles as facilitating stewards who are concerned about the benefit of the whole (the couple or family) rather than the promotion of the parts (individual ambition being an example of a "part"). Greenleaf's model takes the burden of responsibility off of one sole leader in the relationship and shares the power and responsibilities among the partners. If in fact one spouse becomes the "chief leader" in any area of the relationship, he or she also becomes the chief servant.

Another important distinction about a servant leadership marriage is that it is built on three essential elements: trust, respect, and love. First, trust is not just given but must be earned. Each spouse learns to trust the other after a series of consistent patterns and favorable outcomes. Trust involves keeping one's word even when it hurts. It involves the matching up of one's "who" (who one says he or she is) and one's "do" (what he or she does as expressed through his or her behavior).

> *Couples choose to communicate critical needs and subsequently choose their responses rather than being passive victims of their circumstances.*

Second, respect is the decision to affirm, honor, and recognize a person's inherent worth regardless of the person's previous accomplishments or failures. Respect is not contingent upon desired results but on the value of the individual. Author Dr. Emerson Eggerichs states that often women stop giving respect when they feel unloved, and men stop giving love when they feel disrespected (Eggerichs, 2004). Although respect is something that men tend to value more heavily, it is something that is important to both genders.

Third, love comes in many different forms (i.e. philos, eros, agape), but here we are referring to agape love or unconditional, sacrificial love. This refers to a love where one is not just in the relationship for what one can get, but rather what one can give. This kind of love provides the security and safety that helps partners in the relationship thrive rather than merely survive. This love acknowledges the strengths and weaknesses of one's partner and still chooses to accept him or her while contributing to the overall growth and development of that individual. This love is a true servant leadership love.

The Habits of Servant Leadership Marriages

To emphasize the practices or "habits" of a servant leadership marriage, we will apply Stephen Covey's 7 Habits of Highly Effective People as a framework. These habits highlight servant leadership principles. The first habit focuses on being proactive and choosing our responses versus being a victim. A servant leadership marriage practices being honest and upfront with your partner regarding your wishes, desires, and preferences rather than being passive aggressive or a martyr. Couples choose to communicate critical needs and subsequently choose their responses rather than being passive victims of their circumstances.

A second habit of servant leadership marriages is "beginning with the end in mind." Couples must decide in advance how they want their marriage lived out, while asking a number of questions: What is our vision for our marriage and what is its purpose? What is our marriage mission statement? Although most couples don't plan on getting a divorce when they marry and yet approximately half do, how will we keep our marriage together? What safety nets are we going to put in place to protect our marriage from issues such as infidelity, abuse, lack of communication, or debt? When all is said and done, what type of marriage do we envision and how will we take the necessary steps to carry out our vision to fruition?

Third, the couple has to put first things first. Covey talks about doing what is important versus what is urgent. Throughout the seasons of a marriage, many "urgencies" will occur that scream for a couple's time, attention, and resources. The couple, however, has to prioritize what is most important to them, their relationship, and marriage above and beyond the needs of their children, careers, and community demands. This does not mean that they need to neglect these areas, but the bottom line is that they must consistently do what is best for them as a couple first, parents second, and professionals last. Otherwise, they may wake up one day with a big house and great kids but a lifeless marriage.

A fourth habit of servant leadership marriages is that they constantly think win-win. If a decision is not good for one partner, then it's not good for either of them. Since the couple is a team, all of their efforts must produce long-term benefits for the whole rather than just the parts. This does not mean that sacrifices are never made on the part of individual members, but it suggests that each partner must be thinking about the overall well-being of the marriage/family rather than strictly selfish gain. A question might be, "How does this career move impact my spouse's career and/or social ties?" This suggests thinking as a "we" instead of as a "me." The goal should always be optimal long-term winning for the team.

A fifth habit has to do with effective communication. Servant leadership marriages seek to understand first rather than seeking to be understood. It focuses on serving one's partner by choosing to clearly hear and listen to him or her before responding. This involves "active listening." Active listening involves listening first, restating what you have heard, and asking if you heard your partner correctly before responding. Taking the time to hear one's partner is a key element in building trust, respect, and love. It is crucial to being a servant leader and a good marriage partner.

> If a decision is not good for one partner, then it's not good for either of them.

The sixth habit is to "synergize." Synergizing involves team work—sharing ideas and resources, being emotionally available, and realizing that each part contributes to the whole. A marriage can only be as strong as its individual partners. If both people in the marriage are happy and whole, the marriage will be happy and whole. If both people are contributing to the well-being of their home team, then the home will be strong. When couples work together and are in tune with their partner's needs, the outcome is an effective and thriving marriage.

The seventh habit is taking time to "sharpen the saw." Every couple, no matter how loving and happy, must take time away from their routine life to nurture, repair, and rebuild the walls of their marriage. This is true service. For some, this may be taking part in marriage counseling, being involved in a periodic marriage retreat, taking a vacation without the kids, scheduling a regular date night, reading books on improving one's marriage, or being mentored by an older couple. Good marriages are no accident. Servant leadership marriages are intentional and make having a healthy and vibrant marriage a priority.

Conclusion

Greenleaf's model of servant leadership

can be applied beyond the corporate and non-profit levels to the social and structural levels of marriages and relationships.

> *When couples work together and are in tune with their partner's needs, the outcome is an effective and thriving marriage.*

Servant leadership marriages produce high rewards but require going countercultural to modern society and making a commitment to put someone else above oneself. It suggests that good marriages don't just happen by accident, but require an attitude of a servant. This chapter has examined the habits of servant leadership marriages that are practiced as a daily commitment to building strong and enduring relationships. As we return to the virtue of service in our relationships and marriages, we will see the fruits of our marriages and families impacting not only our homes, but those of our children, our communities, and our society as a whole.

PERSONAL REFLECTION EXERCISE

1. Identify two marriages you have observed that follow the servant leader marriage principles. Write about the positive impact of those principles in the lives of the couples who follow them.

2. Identify three things you can do or will start doing to develop a servant leadership marriage or relationship. Spell out any difficulties you will have in doing these things, as well as the positive impact you hope they will have.

SMALL GROUP LEARNING TASK

Form a small group of no more than four. Create a Y chart of how the servant leader marriage can approach the issues of money, sex, and power.

A Servant Leader Approach to Marriage

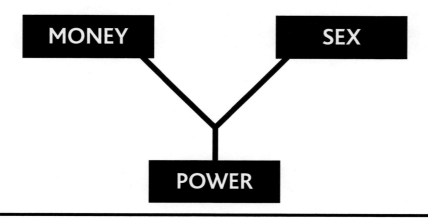

REFERENCES

Covey, S. 1992. *Principle-Centered Leadership.* New York: Fireside.

Covey, S. 1989. *7 Habits of Highly Effective People.* New York: Simon & Schuster.

Eggerichs, E. 2004. *Love & Respect.* Colorado Springs, CO: Focus On the Family/Integrity.

Greenleaf, R. 2002. *Servant Leadership.* New York: Paulist Press.

The Art of Finishing Well:

Paul as Servant Leader

by Grace Preedy Barnes

Summary: Following Paul's formula will enable us to initiate effective leadership pathways and to finish well.

Acts 18:1-28 and 20:17-38

My father, Clarence Preedy, was a British pioneer-style missionary with the China Inland Mission back in the 1930s. He and my mother were both raised as missionary kids in China. They met in China, my father from England and my mother from the United States. Their children, the four of us, were also raised as MKs (missionary kids), three of us born in China, one in the Philippines during World War II, where we were captured and held for over three years. Following the war and some rest time in the United States and England, we eventually returned to China until the Communists took over. Our father, held for three years until he was finally released, joined us in the United States during the 1950s. My parents finally settled in the United States, working with a couple other mission organizations, teaching and working in their training schools. My dad eventually died at the age of 86. I was privileged to be with him during the last week of his life. During a conversation about our family, I was able to tell him the impact he had had on my life. Because of our many separations, his war experiences, and his own tendency to be a private person, he often felt he was not a good father. In many ways he was not ideal, but the way he lived his life, his principles, and his commitments to God and to China were exemplary. He taught many young people with his life, preaching and teaching both in Bible school courses and missionary boot-camp training. After his death we found that he had been corresponding with about 300 people, many of who were former students and whom he had discipled and mentored both in person and through letters. He continued to be about God's work till the end of his life.

> Paul's farewell address to the elders at Ephesus demonstrates how a leader finishes well.

The passages of Acts 18-20 (Acts 18:1-28 and 20:17-38) about Paul remind me of my dad. Both were strong leaders, plunged daringly into new contexts, faced many tri-

Grace Preedy Barnes, Ph.D. is Professor of Organizational Leadership and Program Director of the Operation Impact at Azusa Pacific University which offers the MAOL degree program worldwide. She has taught in more than 25 countries and traveled to many more along with the 50+ faculty who travel to teach up to 600 students per year.

als and sufferings, made mistakes along the way, but were faithful to God's mission until the end. One ought to be able, like Paul, to come to the end of one's life and ministry and be able to rehearse one's integrity.

Studies on leadership in recent decades, however, have shown that biblical, historical, and contemporary leaders do not tend to finish well for a variety of reasons: unexpected difficulties, trials, death of loved ones, moral or discipline problems, disillusionment, learning or growth patterns, and lack of mentoring. In contrast, Paul's farewell address to the elders at Ephesus demonstrates how a leader finishes well (20:17ff.). Even though Paul had sinned boldly as a young man and made mistakes along the way, he demonstrated how he had lived and worked with them. In humility, tears, and empathy, he continually warned them of possible dangers (20:19). He tried to serve them by being helpful and teaching them publicly; traveling house to house he built relationships in various contexts (20:20). He believed he was called to both Jews and Gentiles and was faithful to the gospel of faith in Jesus Christ through repentance (20:21). He was a discipler, a mentor, and a friend. Not only willing to serve but to commit to the unknown, Paul exhorted leaders to watch over the flock as well as themselves. Personal leadership development is as important as leading others and necessary for effective servant leadership (20:25-31). As we will explore later, he provided for his own needs and worked with people incarnationally rather than expecting them to take of his needs. Paul was not a burden to his followers. One of the paradoxes of scripture is the principle that says "in giving we receive" (20:32-35). Paul's leadership model affirms the principles that I gained in my work with

> *Personal leadership development is as important as leading others and necessary for effective servant leadership.*

Young Life. It is important to explore people beneath the surface in the following ways:

1. Go where people are.
2. Win the right to be heard.
3. Learn their language (what communicates to them).
4. Share the gospel in life and words.

Paul's life profoundly influenced the church at Ephesus and its elders. They shared an emotional goodbye, praying and weeping together. He and they knew that danger lay ahead for Paul and that they would not see him again (20:36-38). But Paul knew that he could leave the work in their hands. He knew he could trust them to continue and develop future leaders, as he had done for them. Struggles and persecutions would be a continual part of Paul's life and work. This was promised by the Holy Spirit (20:22-23). Servant leadership is costly, and Paul's followers had seen him handle the difficult situations that came into his life. What a marvelous example for them to follow.

My personal interest in the subject of servant leadership began 20 years ago when I was asked to teach a course entitled "Exploration into Servant Leadership" as part of Azusa Pacific University's overseas master's degree in leadership studies, called Operation Impact, which is offered world wide primarily to missionaries and other Christian workers. In researching this topic I placed myself on the mailing list for such groups as The Robert K. Greenleaf Center, the Servant Society, and the Servant Leadership School at the Church of the Saviour in Washington, D.C. I began to discover a network of people not only interested in living out these ideas but also in applying them to organizational settings.

Even though the concepts of servanthood and leadership were familiar to me and had biblical roots, I was surprised to find that the term "servant leadership" was initiated through the vision and works of Robert K. Greenleaf, who was employed at AT&T for many years. In his later years he became an organizational consultant to educational, business, and religious institutions. Greenleaf once read a story that profoundly affected what he saw as a crisis in leadership. The story that he read was in Hermann Hesse's *Journey to the East*, a book often read by university students during the turbulent times of the late 1960s.

> *In this story we see a band of men on a mythical journey probably also Hesse's own journey. The central figure of the story is Leo who accompanies the party as the servant who does their menial chores, but also sustains them with his spirit and his song. He is a person of extraordinary presence. All goes well unto Leo disappears. Then the group falls into disarray and the journey is abandoned. They cannot make it without the servant Leo. The narrator, one of the party, after some years of wandering finds Leo and is taken into the Order that had sponsored the journey. There he discovers that Leo, whom he had known first as servant, was in fact the titular head of the Order, its guiding spirit, a great and noble leader.[1]*

Greenleaf responded with a desire to serve and began promoting a leadership style in which one leads by serving. Even after his death Greenleaf's books and essays are still being read, and many "followers" are writing about the paradoxical nature of servant leadership.

Greenleaf observed that the idea of the servant is deep in Judeo-Christian heritage. The Bible lists over 1300 references to "servant," "serve," and "service." There are numerous illustrations of servant leadership in the Old and New Testaments. Two types of servant leadership emerge. One seems to represent those on the lower rung or who are the weak in society and are later lifted up like Esther, Rahab, David, Ruth, and Timothy. The more common are those who

> Greenleaf observed that the idea of the servant is deep in Judeo-Christian heritage.

started out on the higher levels of society and were forced into servant learning school by God, either through being sent to the wilderness, being thrown into prison, or being blinded, such as Moses, Joseph, and Paul. Some, like the disciples, had to change course and experience what it meant to serve before they could lead in God's kingdom. Even Jesus spent time in the desert. The scriptural pattern seems to start with servant learning and then is followed by the influence of leadership that comes through experience, maturity, and a desire to serve.

The focus for this chapter is on Paul as servant leader and his philosophy of leadership development that led him to finish his life well. Paul had a great deal of motivation to imitate his primary leadership model, that of Jesus Christ, but he also had freedom to build the church of Christ throughout the world without any previous models outside of Judaism.

Paul Served Alongside Ordinary People (Acts 18:1-23)

In Acts 18:1-3, Paul met and stayed with Aquila and Priscilla, fellow Jews and fellow tentmakers. Paul is depicted working in a secular trade alongside fellow Jewish believers in Christ, providing for his own needs rather than expecting others to support his ministry. He was called to be a partner in God's work; his ability to work at a skill allowed him to live with and identify with common people.[2] Paul served as a steward of God's message. This indicated a life principle from his rabbinic days, when students adopted a trade so that they did not need to depend on their teaching for financial support.[3] In fact, James D.G. Dunn observes: Working with one's hands was quite acceptable in rabbinic circles, but would generally be regarded as beneath the dignity of the well-to-do."[4] Thus, as a servant, Paul counter-culturally placed himself alongside ordinary people. While the reader might assume that Paul roved about looking for people to argue with (18:4), archeology reveals that tentmaking stalls tended to be in or near markets in Corinth, allowing people ample opportunity for Paul to engage with those who passed by or sought to do business. Thus Paul probably shared his faith naturally while at work.[5] This suggests another emerging principle: All work is sacred if done unto the Lord and for God's purposes in this world.

In the religiously pluralistic context of Corinth, Paul entered the synagogues and sought to "convince" Jews and Greeks, but in particular testified to Jews that Jesus was the Messiah (18:4-5). Unfortunately, he received an abusive response and "shook the dust from his clothes," declaring, "Your blood on your own heads!" Then he moved on to the Gentiles (18:6). On the surface one might conclude that Paul did not "finish well" in the Corinthian synagogue. However, Paul maintained in 18:4 what had become an established pattern of going first to the synagogues to provide opportunities for Jews to respond to Christ (18:5; cf. 13:14; 14:1; 17:1-2). Furthermore, after a hostile response, in spite of his harsh rebuke, he began a congregation next door to the synagogue in the house of Titius Justus, likely a Gentile, as indicated by his Roman name (18:7). Moving in next door to the synagogue may not seem the way to make

> *Thus, as a servant, Paul counter-culturally placed himself alongside ordinary people.*

good relations, but the narrative continues in recapping Paul's bold move by stating that the synagogue official, Crispus, "became a believer in the Lord, together with all the household" and that "many of the Corinthians who heard Paul became believers and were baptized" (18:8). Clearly, Paul continued to be a servant of all—Jews and Gentiles.

The text indicates Paul's eagerness to contextualize by entering into the home of a Gentile coupled with Paul's eagerness to continue to minister to Jews of the synagogue. Furthermore, Paul did not cease his pattern of entering into the synagogue in the subsequent cities he would visit (see 18:19). William Neil concludes that Paul's new headquarters in the home of a Gentile beside a hostile synagogue "was not an act of provocation on the part of Paul, but a suitable venue for easy contact with the Gentiles who frequented the synagogue as 'God-fearers.'"[6]

Paul Reproduced Servant Disciples

The city of Corinth, one of the largest, most prosperous, and cosmopolitan cities in Greece in the 50s C.E., contained people who were transient or new, providing Paul with an excellent opportunity to evangelize people from a variety of contexts.[7] Evangelism was not the final word for Paul, however, but the beginning stage of discipleship. After spending a year and a half in Corinth (18:11), Paul made his way back to Antioch, his home base. After spending some time there, "he departed and went from place to place through the region of Galatia and Phrygia, strengthening all the disciples" (Acts 18:23). In "strengthening all the disciples," Paul modeled the Christian lifestyle and encouraged others by revisiting and reinforcing the believers who had become part of the churches during his earlier mission journey. This produced a reproduction and multiplication of disciples. Paul's disciples also modeled and reproduced, becoming "an example to all the believers in Macedonia and in Achaia," as indicated in I Thessalonians 1:7-8, so that "the word of the Lord has sounded forth from you not only in Macedonia and Achaia, but in every place your faith in God has become known."

In several introductions to his epistles Paul refers to himself as an apostle or as a servant of Christ Jesus and refers at times to Timothy and himself as servants. It thus appears that in Paul's mind an apostle was also a servant. This brings the aspects of servant and leader together. He named his disciples as co-authors and co-servants with him in his letters. There does not seem to be a sense of hierarchy in Paul's writings. Rather, he assumes that an apostle or leader is also a servant of Jesus Christ. His high sense of calling to serve was what seemed to propel him to endure a multitude of afflictions and misunderstandings. He drew people alongside him in this calling. We know from his letters that Paul and his multiplying network of disciples specifically encouraged others to serve the Lord, each other, and strangers:

> *Let love be genuine; hate what is evil, hold fast to what is good; love one another with mutual affection; outdo one another in showing honor. Do not lag in zeal, be ardent in spirit, serve the Lord. Rejoice in hope, be patient in suffering, persevere in prayer. Contribute to the needs of the saints, extend hospitality to strangers. (Romans 12:9-13)*

Paul Empowered Male and Female Disciples as Servant Leaders (Acts 18:24-26)

Two of Paul's Corinthian disciples, Priscilla and Aquila, while faithfully attending the synagogue, heard Apollos speak eloquently of the scriptures and Jesus with burning enthusiasm. But Apollos "knew only the baptism of John" (Acts 18:25). So Priscilla and Aquila "took him aside and explained the Way of God more accurately" (18:26). Priscilla's name occurs before Aquila's in the context of teaching a prominent man. The translators of the King James Version, unable to cope with a woman's leadership role in explaining God's truth

Evangelism was not the final word for Paul, however, but the beginning stage of discipleship.

more accurately to a man, reversed the order and put Aquila's name first. However, in the Greek, and reflected in modern translations, Priscilla's name appears first. This demonstrates that Paul not only was a servant to all but allowed women and men to serve together, to teach and even prophesy to one another in the context of community, whether male or female (cf. I Cor. 11:5; Gal. 3:26-29; Acts 21:8-9). Just as Paul empowered men for ministry, so he empowered women. The empowerment came through the work of the Holy Spirit and the practice of spiritual gifts (see Rom. 12; Eph. 4:11-16; I Cor. 12; I Tim. 4:14). His emphasis on the Holy Spirit is evident in the next chapter of Acts, when Paul passed through Ephesus and discovered disciples who had not received the Holy Spirit when they became believers. Then he laid hands on them, and they began to practice the spiritual gifts, in this case tongues and prophecy (19:1-6). Paul emphasized striving for and excelling in spiritual gifts that build up the church (I Cor. 14:12). The use of spiritual gifts to build up and empower others is consistent with Paul's emphasis on service to the body of Christ. Paul selected leaders according to giftedness rather than position and title.

Paul's evident focus on being a servant apostle (leader) of God on behalf of others is supported and endorsed by some of the more current writings about Paul. For example, in 1993 the Evangelical Covenant Church in the United States published a two-volume series entitled Servant Leadership as a review on the subject of authority and governance referencing Paul's writings as part of the foundational basis for discussing leadership today. It expresses that "the New Testament emphasis on servanthood is one of the most consistent and overarching components of the Christian message" and observes that "servant texts that were understood as referring to Jesus are elsewhere in the New Testament applied to Paul and other Christians." It further states that

> It thus appears that in Paul's mind an apostle was also a servant.

> such servant living is not limited to the laity; it is required first of leaders, not as some special feat or task, but only as one example of what is required of every believer. servant Leadership is merely the application of the dynamic of the gospel to the task of leadership.[8]

We have observed that authentic ministry occurs in the service of the gospel by the entire body of Christ through the gifts of the church that edify the church within particular contexts. Authority and leadership, as demonstrated and delegated by Paul, are not based on fixed structures or lofty titles but on an incarnational presence in relational contexts of ministry.[9]

Paul's ability to teach, equip, and turn over? was evident throughout his church-planting days. His model is a catalyst for the servant leadership focus on the group and its ownership. Roland Allen eloquently expresses Paul's ability to lead in this way by example:

> He [Paul] did not establish a constitution, he inculcated principles. He did not introduce any practice to be received on his own or any human authority, he strove to make his converts realize and understand its relation to Christ. He always aimed at convincing their minds and stirring their consciences. He never sought to enforce their obedience by decree; he always strove to win their heartfelt approval and their intelligent cooperation. He never proceeded by command, but always by persuasion. He never did things for them, he always left them to do things for themselves. He set them an example according to the mind of Christ, and he was persuaded that the Spirit of Christ in them would teach them to approve that example and inspire them to follow it.[10]

Discipleship means to serve one another in love. Every member was responsible for each other. This was revolutionary. Greatness was achieved through service. Paul built on the concepts of Jesus and further developed the idea of service:

> His [Paul's] aim was to confirm, encourage, and strengthen the fellowship....It was not to rebuke or to show his authority or to have his personal way. It is unfair to Paul to picture him as a stern man who had no feeling for the deep needs of people. The Corinthians admitted that he was humble when he was with them....He was careful not to give commands."[11]

Servant Leadership Gives Credibility

In The Servant as Leader Greenleaf identified servant leaders as those who are seekers, listeners, able to withdraw and reorient themselves, accepting, tolerant of imperfection, having a sense of the unknowable, intuitive, live by faith, have foresight; they are disturbers and awakeners, healers; they create dangerously and are fully human. "The servant leader is functionally superior" because the servant leader "is closer to the ground," and "hears things, sees things, knows things" with intuitive and exceptional insight that makes the servant leader "dependable and trusted."[12] Paul, I believe, exemplified these characteristics in his life and in the way he developed his ministry with people.

In 1987 Mark V. Attard, Procurator General, gave an inspirational address in which he identified the great leader as a "servant" foremost:

In their own silent, hidden and unobtrusive way, servant leaders get things done while making the followers feel that they accomplished it all by themselves....servant leaders influence through example and convince by their presence...characterized by interdependence, mutual responsibility, collegiality and creativity. It is plural in such a way that interdependent group decision-making becomes a normal process, where communal consensus transcends the individual's opinion and leadership is always exercised with others in a corporate way. It is such leadership that sustains trust and guarantees credibility.[13]

I believe that Paul demonstrated this style of leadership when he established churches, selected and trained leaders, and left them to govern themselves. Paul's impressive servant leadership-style farewell to the Ephesian elders in Acts 20: 17-38 was given at a ripe time in his ministry. He, like all leaders, had to attend "servant learning school," first, making mistakes and learning from them, then going on to make his ulti-

mate contribution. He finished his life well and gave us a full example of what it meant to be a servant leader. Acts concludes with a powerful statement of Paul's relentless servant leadership approach. It states that Paul lived in Rome two years "at his own expense and welcomed all who came to him, proclaiming the kingdom of God and teaching about the Lord Jesus Christ with all boldness and without hindrance" (28:30-31). Paul's desire to use his own resources and minister among the people whom he evangelized and discipled never waned. Paul inclusively ministered as a servant to all who would come to see him. "Finishing well" was not merely an ending but a new beginning. True, Paul had prevailed in the face of the most feared powers of Rome, antagonistic religious leaders, and the realm of the demonic. But Acts does not conclude in idealistic triumph. It concludes

> Just as Paul empowered men for ministry, so he empowered women.

with Paul finishing well, but with an unfinished task. Acts concludes with anticipation of the next phase of mission in which Paul's multiplying disciples throughout large regions of the world would continue to carry out the same mission after his death.

Today's worldwide, unprecedented growth of the church challenges us to "welcome all" who come to us in our global villages and to proclaim boldly "the kingdom of God and teaching about the Lord Jesus." If we do this well, in the spirit of servanthood, then what we finish on this earth becomes a new beginning for a new generation. In summary, Paul's servant leadership included the following:

1. a focus on serving Jesus Christ;

2. a focus on empowering others to serve Jesus Christ and others;

3. being mentored and mentoring others;

4. dealing with tough issues in a personal way;

5. a focus on responsibilities of the body of Christ;

6. participative leadership by persuasion and modeling;

7. the reproductive process of leadership training;

8. a patient process rather than a product orientation;

9. contextualizing within a multi-cultural environment; and

10. finishing well.

Conclusion

Some complex contemporary issues are not addressed in Paul's writings, such as how to apply Paul's principles to groups when they become institutionalized, have established educational and training programs, and have second-generation Christians. In many ways church-planting and para-church groups can apply to Paul's style of mission and church planting more easily because they do not have the bureaucratic barriers and traditions of individuals and institutions that might inhabit growth and development.

While in Brazil with Young Life, we were able to establish a youth ministry with national ownership and leave within a few years. Today, only a sister, and at times advisory, relationship remains. This model has now been duplicated even more speedily in several other Latin American countries. It appears that the reproductive process becomes more complicated with established mission and denominational organizations. "Don't trust the local people to keep the organization going," we were warned. Paul certainly trusted people and empowered them to develop and grow but also to be responsible for the consequences of their ownership. Paul's revolutionary style of servant leadership is desperately needed in today's complex, multicultural, urbanized, and changing world. The message that motivated Paul's mission and gave impetus to his strong beliefs in serving Christ and people can be summed up in his own words during his farewell to the Ephesian church: "But I do not count my life of any value to myself, if only I may finish my course and the ministry that I received from the Lord Jesus, to testify to the good news of God's grace" (Acts 20:24). I am challenged to finish my life well by continuing to seek to be a servant leader and partner with God in the work of God's kingdom throughout the world.

> *Paul emphasized striving for and excelling in spiritual gifts that build up the church.*

PERSONAL REFLECTION EXERCISE

Imagine yourself at 70, at a retirement party given in your honor. Throughout your career, you have integrated all the skills you have learned in this class as you have served in major leadership roles in several large organizations. You have also learned many new things about servant leadership over the years.

Who are the key people you have invited to your retirement celebration? What have you learned about servant leadership from each of them?

There is a time of sharing. What are they saying about you?

Now you are to give a speech and you have decided to talk about the scripture from this article, "In giving we receive" (Acts 20:32-35). Write that speech now.

LARGE GROUP LEARNING TASK

Give your speech "In Giving We Receive" to the entire class. Celebrate all you have done with your learning of servant leadership in this class. Celebrate the future you are launching today!

NOTES

[1] Robert K. Greenleaf, *The Servant as Leader* (Indianapolis, Ind.: Robert K. Greenleaf Center, 1970), 1.

[2] Other passages (such as I Cor. 4:12; I Thess. 2:9; 2 Cor. 11:7) indicate Paul's pride in his self-support.

[3] Kenneth O. Gangel and Max Anders, eds., Holman New Testament Commentary: Acts (Nashville, Tenn.: Broadman and Holman, 1998). 303.

[4] James D. G. Dunn, The Acts of the Apostles (Valley Forge, Pa.: Trinity Press International, 1966), 241.

[5] Ibid.

[6] William Neil, The New Century Bible Commentary: The Acts of the Apostles, ed. Ronald E. Clements and Matthew Black (1973; reprinted, Grand Rapids, Mich.: Eerdmans, 1987), 196.

[7] Ben Witherington III, New Testament History: A Narrative Account (Grand Rapids, Mich.: Baker Books, 2001), 271.

[8] Klyne R. Snodgrass, "Your Slaves—on Account of Jesus," in Servant Leadership, vol. 1, ed. James R. Hawkinson and Robert K. Johnston, 9-16 (Chicago: Covenant Publications, 1933), 10.

[9] For more details on this approach, see David M. Scholer, "Patterns of Authority in the Early Church," in Hawkinson and Johnston, Servant Leadership, 1:45-65.

[10] Roland Allen, Missionary Methods: St. Paul's or Ours? (Grand Rapids, Mich.: Eerdmans, 1962), 149.

[11] Dean S. Gilliland, Pauline Theology and Mission Practice (Grand Rapids, Mich.: Baker Books, 1983), 285.

[12] Greenleaf, The Servant as Leader, 32.

[13] Mark V. Attard, "Inspirational Leadership Keynote Address," paper distributed at a servant leadership conference sponsored by the Greenleaf Center, Atlanta, Ga. (June 11, 1987), 6

Instructor's Map

For Facilitating Maximum Learning in Students

by Christine Wood

You hold in your hands a very valuable tool for learning servant leadership. Adults learn by doing, so this is a working book designed to assist students to do the tasks of servant leadership. The importance of this working book is that it gives instructors the opportunity to include in your teaching by lecture also teaching by practical experience. The articles are placed in a flexible sequential order. By the time your students have finished all the exercises in this working book, they will have learned how to apply the principles of servant leadership to their personal lives, their secular jobs, their Christian ministry, their civic responsibilities, their marriages, and other significant relationships.

They will learn through a two fold process of Personal Reflection Exercises and Small Group Learning Tasks. The Personal Reflection Exercises are to be done either prior to class or as a silent exercise in class. Regardless of which way you choose to do it, what would be ideal is if you could allot an extra 15 minutes in their small group to share their discoveries from their journal exercises.

The Small Group Learning Tasks will generally take about 30 minutes of class time. There are exceptions to this, specifically Article 7 and Article 12. The last article of this working book has a Large Group Learning Task which is a whole class celebration of learning.

Adult educators are learning that it's essential to include a step beyond group discussion, thus we have made an emphasis in this working book on using charts. This will take your adult learners beyond "discussion" to "doing" the material they are reading. You will need charts, wide felt tip pens, and wall space in your class room for these charts. An additional benefit of using them is that your students will observe a visual sign of their work of learning servant leadership. Gallery Walks are done by having students walk by the charts and pause as a spokesperson from the chart being viewed teaches the rest of the class what that small group discovered. In Gallery Walks students teach each other and we have discovered that students have astute insights and are empowered as they share their discoveries with their peers.

Since engagement is essential in adult learning, your Small Group Learning Tasks require students to form small groups of three or four. The reason we specified group size is for maximum participation. Our formula for this is based on research that reveals that almost everyone will share in a small group of four, but in groups of five or more it's usually the most articulate and extroverted who will actively participate. We're confident that if you keep these small groups to a maximum of four you will watch your whole class engage in learning.

NOTES

NOTES

NOTES